Think Like
Jesus

❧

Think Like Jesus

BY GEORGE BARNA

INTEGRITY®
PUBLISHERS
Nashville

THINK LIKE JESUS

Published by Integrity Publishers, a division of Integrity Media, Inc.,
5250 Virginia Way, Suite 110, Brentwood, TN 37027.

HELPING PEOPLE WORLDWIDE EXPERIENCE *the* MANIFEST PRESENCE *of* GOD.

Published in association with Yates & Yates, LLP, Literary Agents, Orange, California.

Unless otherwise indicated, Scripture quotations are taken from the *Holy Bible,* New
Living Translation, copyright © 1996. Used by permission of Tyndale House
Publishers, Inc., Wheaton, Illinois 60189. All rights reserved.

Scripture quotations indicated KJV are from the King James Version of the Bible.

Cover Design: David Uttley
             UDG | Designworks
             www.udgdesignworks.com
Interior: Inside Out Design & Typesetting

Library of Congress Cataloging-in-Publication Data

Barna, George
Think like Jesus: make the right decision every time / by George Barna.
   p.   cm.
Includes bibliographical references.

ISBN 1-59145-019-5 (hardcover)
ISBN 1-59145-123-X (international paperback)

1. Christian Life. 2. Decision making—Religious aspects—Christianity. I. Title.
BV4509.5.B373   2003
248.4—dc21   2003008207

Printed in the United States of America
03 04 05 06 07 RRD 9 8 7 6 5 4 3 2 1

Contents

─── ❧ ───

Contents

PART 3:
PRACTICING A BIBLICAL WORLDVIEW

Acknowledgments

———— ❧ ————

Life is often a study in opposites. This book is an example. On the one hand, this has been one of the most enjoyable and challenging books I've written, allowing me to spend numerous hours examining the Bible and reflecting on its truths and principles and how they fit together into a comprehensive and coherent perspective. On the other hand, this has been the most difficult book I have ever written, pushing me way outside my comfort zone to fulfill a calling I keenly feel but which scares me nevertheless.

Given the challenges, pressures, tensions, and fears related to this project, the resulting book could not have been completed without the active and invaluable participation of a diverse group of supporters.

A variety of friends and colleagues provided assistance ranging from theological perspectives and manuscript reflections to spiritual support through prayer and encouragement. Such help came from Henry Blackaby, Chuck Colson, Connie and David DeBord, Gary and Catherine Greig, Chuck and Jeanette Laird, Kevin and Kathy Mannoia, Steve Russo, Danny Sartin, and John and Pam Saucier. Thank you for blessing me so profusely with your wisdom and enthusiasm.

My colleagues at Barna Research helped out in many ways. I am thankful to Irene Castillo, Lynn Gravel, Cameron Hubiak, Pam Jacob, David Kinnaman, Dan Parcon, Celeste Rivera, and Kim Wilson for their gracious support.

ACKNOWLEDGMENTS

My publishing team played a significant role in the development of the final product. Specifically, I am indebted to Anita Palmer of Sam Hill Editorial Services for her flexibility as well as for her encouragement and sensitive editing; to Sealy and Curtis Yates for their representation of my work to the publishing community; and to my friends at Integrity Publishers. In particular, Joey Paul was instrumental in helping to guide this project, and Byron Williamson shared the vision for this material.

My most beloved support group is my family. They paid a big price to allow me to wrestle through this material. My wife, Nancy, deserves all the credit in the world for encouraging me, reading draft after draft, keeping the world at bay in order to protect my writing bubble, and juggling more family and company responsibilities than were reasonable during the writing period. My daughters, Samantha and Corban, cheerfully encouraged me throughout the project and refrained from making me feel guilty for not spending as much time with them as all of us desired. I pray that God will bless them in abundant ways for their selfless support of my attempt to help people know, love, and serve our Lord more significantly.

In the end, I am most grateful to God for giving me the opportunity, the ability, the physical strength and the spiritual protection to complete this book. May its impact advance His ways and His kingdom.

Introduction

Did I Miss Something?

THE FORTY-FIVE-MINUTE DRIVE from Ventura to the Santa Barbara Airport is one of my enjoyable escape routes. Flying these days is drudgery, but it seems less torturous when your passage to the airport is so scenic. Most of my drive offers spectacular views of the Pacific Ocean under cloudless blue skies and a blazing sun that glistens off the rolling waves, reminding me of the Creator's beauty. A recent Monday morning sojourn to the airport followed that description to a T.

My post-drive mellow attitude survived the usual airport hassles, and I boarded the small jet that would deliver me to Dallas. I strapped myself in, removed a hardback volume about leadership from my briefcase, and began to lose myself in the book. I couldn't help but notice my seatmate, though: The young man carried on an animated conversation with two casually clad buddies in the row behind us. They behaved like a trio of college fraternity brothers, swapping snide comments about work colleagues and fantasizing about the barhopping they anticipated in Dallas.

The Conversation

Halfway into the flight, my reading was interrupted by the flight attendant's offer of a beverage to complement the skimpy bag of peanuts provided as sustenance. Bored with his peers, my seatmate seized the opportunity to engage me in conversation.

"Reading for work?" he asked with a knowing smile.

An intense introvert by nature, I dread such small talk with strangers I am likely never to see again. But, knowing that my faith in Jesus Christ is meant to be shared in ways that leave a positive influence on the lives of others, I have made peace with such experiences and recognize that God may have a purpose for the engagement. Nothing happens by accident, so perhaps there was a deeper purpose for this encounter. With some emotional discomfort and spiritual anticipation, I entered the fray.

"Yeah."

Okay, I didn't enter it with much gusto, but it was a start.

"What's it about?" my inquisitive junior asked.

"It's about the spiritual dynamics of leadership development. I work with leaders to try to help them maximize their skills and abilities. Books like this help me know what other developers of leaders are discovering about how to do that more effectively."

The introvert in me was proud of having strung together three coherent sentences on my favorite topic. But, hey, give me a break: at least I had refrained from smothering my seatmate with Christianese before he took the first sip of his five-dollar vodka and tonic.

"Huh. What kind of leaders do you work with?"

There it was, the question that had killed a thousand conversations before. But, I reasoned, if God is in control—and there is no doubt in my mind that He always has been and always will be—then honesty is the best policy.

"Mostly with pastors of Christian churches. I own a small marketing research firm that specializes in church-related work, and I spend most of my time trying to help pastors and other church people serve God as effectively as possible."

Answers like that are always the turning point in these blind conversations. You'd be surprised how many people recoil with horror once they realize that I am apparently a devoted Christian—probably a *Jesus freak.* They develop a sudden fixation with the clouds outside the tiny window next to their seat. Others assume the glazed-eye look of someone who has just been exposed to a painfully detailed account of the IRS code regarding proper inventory-control accounting procedures. Occasionally someone will respond with excitement, for they are fellow disciples of Jesus and know they can now enjoy a more meaningful personal connection with me. And a very few are non-evangelicals who are genuinely intrigued by the notion of a seemingly intelligent person being a devoted follower of Christ, and they actually decide to continue the conversation.

My seatmate apparently was one of the latter. My goal of finishing the book by touchdown faded. But God obviously had something in mind and, frankly, I was more than a bit curious to see what it was.

PLUNGING IN

We introduced ourselves. He was Bill, from Las Vegas, on a business trip related to his job with a major accounting firm. Bill had been employed there for nearly four years and was on the fast track to upper management. With the pleasantries out of the way, he plunged ahead.

"So, you're, like, uh . . . a Christian, huh?"

"Yeah, my faith has become the focal point of my life."

"Hey, well, I'm a Christian, too," Bill proclaimed, looking earnestly at me. "I mean, I don't go to church and all, but I was raised as a Christian and went when I was a kid. But I don't really believe in God anymore."

Given my deep personal conviction that God not only exists but hears every word we say, my heart started racing at Bill's confession of unfaith. But because I oversee a ministry that interviews more than ten thousand people each year regarding faith matters, statements like Bill's are a dime a dozen; consequently, they lose their shock value. So, while I felt an immediate twinge of despair for Bill, I recognized the importance of his admission and began to have a sense of what God's purpose for this conversation might be.

"Really? You don't believe in God? Why not?"

"Well, He may exist, but I just think there's too much needless suffering and hardship in the world to buy into what my church taught me. You know, God being love, and all that crap. It doesn't make sense, does it?"

Now, I love God with all my heart, mind, strength, and soul, but I shiver with fear and self-doubt when I enter such dialogues. Who am I to speak for the living God? What do I know about the totality of Scripture? Why should anyone give a toot in the wind about what I believe? What others—and I—really need is simply to think like Jesus, to see the world and its complexities and nuances from His point of view.

Despite my insecurities, however, I usually bludgeon ahead, secure in the realization that the history of humanity conveys a pattern of one person affecting the life of another through relationship, communication, and love. Admittedly, though, it's at these moments when I suddenly rediscover the meaning of *fervent prayer*—and thank God that my eternal destiny is not dependent upon my ability to provide the perfect theological treatise.

I responded to Bill's question quietly, not wanting to sound belligerent or arrogant. "Actually, it makes a lot of sense to me. Just because some people prosper and others suffer doesn't negate the existence or character of God," I said. I added that suffering is sometimes a means to a better end, and that God uses it to draw people closer to Him or to give others who are more fortunate a chance to serve those in need. "But this is interesting. So, if you don't believe in God, then how do you explain things like the existence of the universe?"

Bill nestled into his seat cushion and began to expand on how he views the world. "I can buy the big bang theory. But, really, it doesn't matter much. What matters is the here and now. Maybe there is a god out there, but he's really not part of my life. I have to take control of my

Introduction

life and steer it to the right place. Things are going well for me. I'm on that fast-track program"—he had briefly alluded to this during our introductions and was clearly proud of that status—"and I'm getting my family life together."

"You're married?"

"Was. Just got divorced eight months ago, after five years together. We have one daughter, so I stay in Vegas to be near her. It's all working out well." The frown on his face belied that assessment.

I asked him if, without God, he thought there are moral absolutes, ways of distinguishing right from wrong.

"Of course," he guffawed, aghast that I might think he was a moral anarchist. "You don't need God to know there have to be limits. I live a good, moral life, and I teach those values to my daughter."

"But if there is no God, then what's the basis of right and wrong in your belief system?" I asked, hoping he might begin to see the problem with his position.

"You just know what's right and wrong. I mean, you can feel it, right? You know from experience what works and what doesn't work, and you kinda build a mental catalogue of do's and don'ts based on those experiences. And you see it played out in movies and on TV, where they pretty much contrast the different ways you can deal with situations and show the different outcomes of each approach. Heck, the world is filled with examples of right and wrong, and if you're sensitive to it, you can easily tell what's good and what's bad."

These were some interesting sources of moral authority: feelings, experience, movies and television. "So, in other words, you're saying that everyone has to make up his own mind about what is morally right or wrong?"

"Definitely!" Bill exclaimed, taking another draw from his drink and pausing to look out the window at the billowing clouds beneath our aircraft.

If we all do what we believe is right, Bill said, it all works out because we're all doing the best we can. "Nobody's perfect. But if we try our hardest and respect each other, it works. Life is just controlled chaos. There's a type of grand symmetry to life that brings everything into balance if you act with good intent."

By this time it was evident that Bill frequently engaged in these kinds of convoluted barroom conversations. But it was also clear that not many people challenged his views during those interactions.

"But Bill, suppose you say it's okay to kill your ex-wife because she's brought you misery and it's because of her that your daughter no longer lives with you. I come along and say no, killing your wife is immoral. Am I supposed to respect your choice to kill her because she did something you didn't like? What if I then say, 'Sorry, friend, but if that's your final choice, it conflicts with mine, so now I have to kill you first in order to protect that innocent woman.' Am I right to do that? Are you right to kill your ex? Who or what is the final arbiter of all this?"

He started to squirm in his seat—not unreasonable, given the tight fit, but I sensed his fidgeting was the result of something other than physical discomfort.

"You know, you just have to deal with the situation, George. Naw, you shouldn't kill me, and I probably shouldn't kill my ex-wife." He paused, then grinned and continued, "Although there have been times that the thought of nailing her and that lawyer of hers have crossed my mind." He laughed at his repartee, hoping to lighten the conversation and move it to a different plane. I was happy to move to a different point.

Questioning Authority

"I guess what you're really addressing has to do with truth, don't you think? Is there a source of moral truth? When you were growing up, in your church, you probably heard that the Bible is the source of all moral truth. Does the Bible fit into your thinking at all?"

"Well sure, I believe the Bible is a good book; it's got some good stuff in there," Bill said tentatively. Obviously, he was not completely confident in his statement. "I read the Bible sometimes; it's kind of, you know . . . inspiring or challenging."

"But would you say that everything in the Bible is true and accurate?"

"No way," he stated with renewed confidence, straightening in his seat. "There's a lot of historical information that has been proven to be inaccurate, and a lot of the stories are clearly allegories and illustrations, but not real. It has some helpful lessons, though," he finished, perhaps trying to throw me a bone in the hope of getting me to ask some easier questions.

But I was moving on to the big one.

Getting to the Point

"So if the Bible does not provide you with moral absolutes, and its content is not accurate and reliable, then how do you figure out the meaning and purpose of life? What's life about for you, Bill? Why bother getting out of bed in the morning?"

Bill's quick response was evidence he had thought about this question before, to his credit.

"Life is about doing what makes you happy and achieving whatever you can and getting what is due you. When you die, it's over, so you've got to make the best of this life while you can and enjoy whatever opportunities come your way. You've got to live in the moment, because that's all you've got."

We both paused for a few moments, him stirring the remaining ice cubes in his nearly extinct vodka-and-tonic, and me staring at the cover of the book still clutched in my hands. I think we both were evaluating the wisdom of continuing the conversation. Sensing God nudging me forward, I figured I had nothing to lose and perhaps there was something for each of us to gain by moving ahead.

"So, when you die, it's over. That sounds like you don't believe in life after death."

"Oh, I believe in Heaven," he said. I noticed he didn't mention Hell. "You move on to a new form of experience, whatever it is."

"Like reincarnation?"

"Maybe," he offered, noncommittal. "We can't really know what will happen after this life, but I think it will be a place of peace and tranquility."

I had to ask the obvious question. "Bill, if there's no God and there are no rules by which we play the game of life, and the ultimate purpose is to maximize what we do here on earth—who created that place of peace and tranquility, and why bother with any further experience?"

He turned his gaze back out the window. "I don't know. I'm not really worried about life after death. I've got enough on my plate here on earth," he replied.

Turning the Tables

I could tell Bill was starting to get agitated by the constant questioning. Before I could back off he took the offensive, perhaps as much for relief from scrutiny as for interest in my thoughts.

"What about you? What do you say to all of this? You probably have some thoughts on it, huh?"

So far the conversation had been pleasant enough, but I sensed that Bill was feeling defensive and emotionally uncomfortable. The questions were cutting a bit deep for his sense of ease. I figured a summary statement might be in order.

"Well, these are all pretty important questions to me. I hope I didn't offend you by asking question after question," I said.

"No problem," he said.

I went on to share what amounts to my basic statement of faith.

"But to answer your question, I guess I do come at things differently than you. I believe that God exists and has always existed and is in total control of all of creation. The Bible is the document that helps me understand things better. Everything it says seems to add up for me—

and to have proven itself in my own life and experience. It tells me life is a gift from God, and the real bottom line to life is to have a meaningful relationship with Him and to serve Him and others. It all comes together if we follow His moral guidelines—and it really unravels pretty quickly and profoundly if we don't. He gives us the freedom to choose to know and serve Him or to pursue different paths, and that's what causes a lot of the anguish and hardship we undergo."

Bill appeared to be listening to my soliloquy with polite if not rapt attention, so I went on.

I told him that I feel released from many of the pressures my friends feel because of what Jesus did on earth. He looked puzzled.

"I believe that God sent Jesus to earth on my behalf—and yours. Jesus died in order for me to be restored to God. By embracing Jesus' death for my faults, I'm assured of a place in God's presence—Heaven, if you will—after I die."

I said that in the meantime, I try to understand what Jesus was like and to imitate His ways. I fall short more often than not, but God seems to understand that weakness and encourages me to keep trying, keep improving. That's the relationship part—Him guiding, encouraging, understanding, disciplining, rewarding—all the stuff you'd expect in a true relationship: honesty, joy, disappointment, love.

"So, I don't have it all worked out, but the Bible really helps me get closer to the truth. And God intervenes when He needs to—to spare me or redirect me. I'd have to say that my decision to be a follower of Jesus and to try to be more like Him has been the best decision I've ever made."

I had tried to boil my thinking down to a few key points, hoping that something might click in Bill's mind or heart, igniting a desire to explore the thought more intensely. After I finished, he waited a few seconds, stared at his hands, then surprised me with his response.

"Yeah, I know what you mean," he began. "I think I'm in a good place with God. I don't have it all figured out, either, but it's coming. In the end, it will all work out. What do they say, 'I'm a work in progress,' right?"

He chuckled, I smiled, and then we did what two guys always do. We talked about sports.

Loose Connections

Later, after landing, retrieving my luggage, and signing for the keys to a rental car, I replayed the conversation with Bill in my mind as I drove toward my hotel. I kept catching myself, thinking, *He didn't really say that, did he?*

My talk with Bill had been the latest example of how profoundly superficial, illogical, and spiritually deceived many Americans have become. Bill's worldview, his ideology and theology, was internally inconsistent, morally vacuous, and intellectually threadbare—and pretty representative of how so many Americans, especially younger people, think these days. It was a mishmash of existentialism, nihilism, Christian theism, Eastern mysticism, and postmodernism. If I had probed, we probably would have uncovered elements of deism and naturalism as well.

It was quite unnerving to replay the conversation and realize that this poor fellow—and millions like him—tries to make sense out of life with such a garbled understanding of reality.

But the experience also drove home several points for me. For instance:

- Everyone has a worldview. Relatively few have a coherent worldview or are able to articulate it clearly.

- Most people don't consider their worldview to be a central, defining element of their life, although it is.

- People spend surprisingly little time intentionally considering and developing their worldview. More often than not, their worldview development process is one of unconscious evolution and acceptance. They allow it to evolve and sum it up this way: "Whatever."

- Americans rarely interact with each other on a substantive level regarding matters and issues that relate to worldview development and clarification. When they do so, they often do not know how to process the interaction or how to progress from their existing position.

As dismayed as I was for Bill, my agonizing did not end there. The airplane discourse was personally disturbing because it put flesh and blood on the research I'd been conducting for the past several years on truth views and worldview perspectives.

Survey after survey has shown that Americans—including a huge majority of born-again Christians and evangelical Christians—lack a biblical worldview. Worst of all, I realized that since I became a believer some two decades ago, nobody had ever taught me how to develop a Scripture-based worldview to guide every facet of my life. Sure, I had attended hundreds of Sunday school and Christian education classes, church services, taken notes at more sermons than I can remember, had received college and graduate-level training on spiritual matters, and had read numerous Christian books on theology, doctrine, and faith-based living. But the experience with Bill forced me to acknowledge that while I was further down the road of worldview clarity, my efforts had not resulted in much ground gained.

Personal Challenge

Because of my exposure to research on Americans' thinking and my concern about the Church in the last several years, I became obsessed with the notion of intentionally developing a meaningful view of life and living consistently with that perspective. This book is a result of that journey—an incomplete, in-process trail that continues today and will continue until the day I die. Your journey will be different than mine, but that adventure is of such huge significance that I am praying my trials and tribulations en route will encourage you to boldly move forward.

Together we will walk through the process that has helped me begin to develop a biblical worldview that affects every facet of my life. In the chapters that follow, we will explore the concept of a worldview, discuss why it matters, examine the most common worldviews that people possess, and delve into how to develop a worldview based on foundational Scriptural principles. I'll describe the research I've been conducting on what people believe and how churches can be a helpful ally in the battle for the mind and heart. After all of this, we'll spend some time thinking through how to apply your worldview to real-world issues and situations.

Perhaps as you read my conversation with Bill you were rehearsing your own answers to some of the questions we tackled and felt a bit uneasy about the state of your worldview. I can assure you that you're not alone. Join me as we do our best to intentionally fashion a worldview that honors God and leads to a more fulfilling and appropriate life. With some focused effort, you and I will be more capable of thinking like Jesus.

Part One

Perspectives on the State of Worldviews

One

What's the Big Deal?

There were three of us still hanging around in the church foyer after a full day of teaching. Of the three hundred or so pastors who had attended the seminar I'd been leading in Charlotte, North Carolina, these last two were talking through discipleship strategies with me when I popped the question.

"So, what do you guys do to help your people get a biblical worldview?"

The taller of the two, balding and with twenty-plus years' experience in the pastorate, wasted no time answering.

"We have missionaries speak in our services several times a year. Every Sunday school class has time set aside to read a brief report and pray about faith-related events happening in other parts of the world. And we have a summer missions trip for families that always fills up quickly," he proclaimed. "We work hard to make sure that they realize the American Church is not the total sum of God's work in the world. Our people get it."

His colleague, a decade his junior and relatively new to the pastorate, took up the baton without missing a beat.

"What we do is preach through the entire Bible every five years. We have all of our teaching venues—the service, the Sunday school classes, the youth groups, even the cell groups—focus on the same passages covered in the sermon that week, ensuring that we give all the key scriptural principles adequate consideration. By the time we're through

3

the cycle, they've been exposed to all of the basic principles of Christianity and will have a biblical worldview."

The two beamed, clearly pleased they were on track. After complimenting each other they turned to me, waiting for words of praise and encouragement. As the seconds ticked by and I continued to gaze at them without responding, their smiles began to fade and curiosity set in. The younger pastor finally asked, "That's what you meant, isn't it?"

GLOBAL PERSPECTIVE OR WORLDVIEW?

I had a disappointing sense of déja vu. I have heard similar replies countless times in the different areas of the United States where I go to teach pastors and to learn from them. Not wanting to offend or discourage them, I tried to ease into my reply.

"Well, those are very helpful activities, for sure. It would be beneficial if more churches helped their people, as you have, to develop a global perspective on God's work and to have regular teaching related to the totality of His Word." I paused, searching for what I hoped would be clear but not disheartening words. "But a biblical worldview is more than that."

I continued with what I prayed would be a persuasive description.

"A biblical worldview is thinking like Jesus. It is a way of making our faith practical to every situation we face each day. A biblical worldview is a way of dealing with the world such that we *act* like Jesus twenty-four hours a day because we *think* like Jesus."

I offered an analogy: "It's like having a pair of special eyeglasses we wear that enables us to see things differently, to see things from God's point of view, and to respond to those perceptions in the way He would prescribe if He were to provide us with direct and personal revelation."

As we continued talking, these two pastors raised questions about a biblical worldview similar to those of other pastors and church leaders with whom I have had such discussions in the past several years. It was

4

clear that even though believers in this nation are in desperate need of a biblical life lens, implementing such a developmental process in churches, schools, homes, and ministries around the country was not going to happen overnight. A lot of foundations need to be put in place first.

WHAT IS THIS "BIBLICAL WORLDVIEW" THING?

For years I was scared off by the term "biblical worldview." It had connotations of breadth and depth that were overwhelming. But the more I realized that my own Christian life was a haphazard series of disjointed choices only marginally and inconsistently influenced by my faith, the more determined I became to get serious about worldview development.

We All Have Worldviews

Once involved in the process, I soon learned that there is no reason to be frightened about the concept of worldview development. Instead I ought to be more worried by the fact that I already had a fully developed and operational worldview that I wasn't even aware of!

While most people never think about their worldview on a conscious level, *everyone has one.* Our moment-to-moment decisions are shaped by the worldview we have adopted and adapted over the course of time, often without realizing that we are dependent upon such a framework for decision making.

Whenever we make a decision, we unconsciously run it through a mental and emotional filter that allows us to make choices consistent with what we believe to be true, significant, and appropriate. That filter is the result of how we have organized information to make sense of the world in which we live.

Without a worldview, we'd be incapable of arriving at many of the hundreds of decisions we make each day because every option would seem just as appealing as every other. To make even minor choices we rely upon our sense of right and wrong, good and bad, useful and useless, appropriate and inappropriate, to produce what we believe are the wisest choices. From our earliest days out of the womb we have been creating this understanding of how life works and the best options to pursue.

A *biblical worldview* is a means of experiencing, interpreting, and responding to reality in light of biblical perspective. This life lens provides a personal understanding of every idea, opportunity, and experience based on the identification and application of relevant biblical principles so that every choice we make may be consistent with God's principles and commands. At the risk of seeming simplistic, it is asking the question, "What would Jesus do if He were in my shoes right now?" and applying the answer without compromising because of how we anticipate the world reacting.

HOW DID JESUS THINK LIKE JESUS?

Jesus was able to model a biblical worldview because He is God and thus knows and embodies truth and rightness. Yet, the fact that He was human during His time of physical presence on earth suggests that He also had to work at maintaining a godly view of everything He encountered. His process was neither accidental nor hidden: His exhortation to His disciples was "Let me teach you."[1] What can we learn from His approach to decision making?

The narrative of Jesus' life gives us a sense that there were four elements working together that facilitated His worldview.

First, He had a *foundation* that was clear, reliable, and accessible. Second, He maintained a laser-beam *focus* on God's will. Third, He evaluated all information and experiences through a *filter* that produced appropriate choices. Fourth, He acted in *faith*.

Jesus' Foundation

What was the implacable foundation of Jesus' thoughts and actions? The holy Word of God as recorded in the Scriptures. Jesus was not content to simply have the Scriptures available at the nearest temple: He memorized key passages in order to gain the guidance and assurance He needed in pivotal moments.[2] Even when He was instructing the disciples He would anchor His teaching to core scriptural principles.[3] When He scolded the religious leaders of the day for their inappropriate decisions, He would challenge their knowledge and interpretation of Scripture.[4]

Jesus' Focus

Jesus in one sense was the definition of narrow-minded: His focus was solely on knowing and fulfilling the will of God. He sought to convey that theme to His followers, informing them, "I have come down from heaven to do the will of God who sent me, not to do what I want."[5] His great knowledge of the Scriptures would have provided Him with the content of His focus, but how was He able to avoid the distractions and lock on to God's will?

Jesus spent time alone with God, seeking solitude to hear the voice of His Father in Heaven.[6] He fasted in order to remind Himself to focus on God.[7] He identified and promoted His God-given mission, seeing that purpose as the priority of His life.[8] He prayed constantly for guidance.[9] The message to us is that when we passionately desire to focus on God, and invest in doing so, God will foster the connection.

Jesus' Filter

Jesus made very different decisions than the norm because He filtered information through a different mental, emotional, and spiritual grid. His filter eliminated assumptions and expectations in favor of a stringent analysis of facts and scriptural principles. A stellar example of that outside-the-box thinking was provided in the Sermon on the Mount. He challenged people's ideas by reminding them, "You have heard . . . " before shredding those erroneous views with a revolutionary "but I say. . . . "[10] Some of His statements reflected simple but profound wisdom drawn from a deep well of discernment, understanding of humanity, and basic biblical perspective.[11]

Jesus' Faith

Jesus' thinking would have been intriguing from a scholarly perspective but powerless without the faith to act upon His views. This insight is lost upon many Christians who know what's right but fail to do what they know. Jesus demonstrates that a genuine biblical worldview must be backed up by action. Such action demands complete faith that doing what honors God, rather than men, is the only yardstick of success.

Jesus' faith was multifaceted. Notice, for instance, that He was realistic, knowing that His efforts to do the will of God would cause Himself hardship and suffering.[12] That realization did not deter Him because He had weighed the alternative—self-directed activity in disobedience to God—and recognized the futility and stupidity of fighting God. He could therefore take what we perceive to be courageous action, but which He perceived to be the only sensible path.[13] He had no anxiety about the consequences because He knew that as long as He honored God and allowed the Holy Spirit to work through Him, His perspectives and choices were appropriate.[14]

Is learning to think like Jesus beyond our grasp? Not at all! God has provided us with all the tools—the foundation, the skills needed to focus and filter, and the means of faith—that enable us to follow Jesus' example.

THINKING LIKE JESUS IS
A MATTER OF OBEDIENCE

The starting point for Jesus was knowing and committing to doing what God commands in the Bible. Thus it would be a good idea to see what the Bible teaches about developing a biblical lens on the world.

It turns out that the Bible speaks loud and clear on this matter. Indisputably, God commands us to think like Jesus. Here are some examples of His admonitions.

Seek God's Wisdom

> Tune your ears to wisdom, and concentrate on understanding. Cry out for insight and understanding. Search for them as you would for lost money or hidden treasure. Then you will understand what it means to fear the LORD, and you will gain knowledge of God. For the LORD grants wisdom! From his mouth come knowledge and understanding. He grants a treasure of good sense to the godly. (Proverbs 2:2–7)

This passage gives deeper meaning to the notion of God's wisdom: It is more than mere witty sayings or helpful suggestions. It is life itself. Calling this wisdom "hidden treasure," Solomon urges us to make its acquisition and application a top priority. God's wisdom is to become the very fiber of our being, and we cannot rest satisfied until we grasp and live in harmony with His expectations. Thankfully, He grants such wisdom to those who truly seek it—but we must pursue it.

Don't Be Fooled

> Don't let anyone lead you astray with empty philosophy and high-sounding nonsense that come from human thinking and from the evil powers of this world, and not from Christ. (Colossians 2:8)

Paul's warning to the Colossian believers cautions us that the world will actively seek to turn our minds in a different direction than that which God intends. If we keep in mind that we are involved in a battle for our hearts, minds, and souls, then this view takes on added significance. In the competitive marketplace of ideas and images, there will be many seductive alternatives awaiting us, many of which will seem reasonable because our enemy disguises evil in attractive packaging. We must carefully consider each option and reject those that do not conform to God's ways.

Commit to What's Important

> If you obey all his laws and commands, you will enjoy a long life. Listen closely. . . . Be careful to obey. Then all will go well with you. . . . The LORD is our God, the LORD alone. And you must love the LORD your God with all your heart, all your soul, and all your strength. And you must commit yourselves wholeheartedly to these commands I am giving you today. Repeat them again and again to your children. Talk about them when you are at home and when you are away on a journey, and when you are lying down and when you are getting up again. Tie them to your hands as a reminder, and wear them on your forehead. Write them on the doorposts of your house and on your gates. (Deuteronomy 6:2–9)

God's words to Moses and the Israelites remind us that building the capacity to think like Jesus is not a one-time, been-there-done-that experience but an endless, winding journey of discovery, revelation, and application. Developing a biblical worldview takes time, mental energy, diligence, and reliance on God's words to us. The content is to be our continual focus and source of reflection. It is a process we are to share with those closest to us, for they are part of our journey of discovery just as we are part of theirs. Our drive to grasp such a worldview is nothing to be bashful about; others ought to observe us and notice that ours is a relentless pursuit of such wisdom and behavior.

Be Transformed

> Don't copy the behavior and customs of this world, but let God transform you into a new person by changing the way you think. Then you will know what God wants you to do, and you will know how good and pleasing and perfect his will really is. (Romans 12:2)

There is no doubt as to God's desire for us: we must intentionally turn our back on the world and aggressively develop a mind the world is incapable of recognizing. We are exhorted to undergo not just a change but a *transformation*. That's what a biblical worldview does to us; it is an intellectual rebirthing of the person akin to the spiritual rebirthing that occurs in our soul when we embrace Christ as our savior.

Fight Appropriately

We are human, but we don't wage war with human plans and methods. We use God's mighty weapons, not mere worldly weapons, to knock down the Devil's strongholds. With these weapons we break down every proud argument that keeps people from knowing God. With these weapons we conquer their rebellious ideas, and teach them to obey Christ. (2 Corinthians 10:3–5)

Alluding to the spiritual warfare in which we are engaged, Paul boldly proclaimed that we are to take on the mind and the weapons of God in order to focus people's attention on right and proper things. To embrace a perspective other than God's is rebellion and leads to spiritual weakness; to take every thought captive for Christ fosters life and obedience.

Rely on God's Guidance

If you need wisdom—if you want to know what God wants you to do— ask him, and he will gladly tell you. He will not resent your asking. But when you ask him, be sure that you really expect him to answer, for a doubtful mind is as unsettled as a wave of the sea that is driven and tossed by the wind. (James 1:5–6)

God wants us to lean on Him for direction and promises to provide such insight if we look to Him for it. But, as James warns us, be ready for supernatural wisdom, not a recitation of what passes for human wisdom. As the prophet Isaiah reminds us (see Isaiah 55:8), His thoughts are not our thoughts—and that's *precisely* why we need to rely upon Him rather than upon our own mind and heart.

Get Fit Spiritually

> Now the Holy Spirit tells us clearly that in the last times some will turn away from what we believe; they will follow lying spirits and teachings that come from demons. . . . Do not waste time arguing over godless ideas and old wives' tales. Spend your time and energy in training yourself for spiritual fitness. . . . Teach these things and insist that everyone learn them. (1 Timothy 4:1, 7, 11)

Should we be surprised that developing and living in harmony with a biblical worldview is unusual in our day? Not at all, according to God. In fact, He foretells the massive numbers of people who will reject His words and instead follow the persuasive albeit false teachings of others. Our responsibility remains the same, in spite of that trend: We are to invest ourselves in being spiritually fit and focused, sharing our insights with those who will listen but majoring on personal spiritual development without excuse.

Pay Attention

> "My thoughts are completely different from yours," says the LORD. (Isaiah 55:8)

As mortal, fallible creations of the living God, we were made in such a way that our natural inclinations will not necessarily coincide with God's. If we wish to have peace with Him, then we must work hard to know, understand, and accommodate His mind and heart. That requires us to be intentional about developing a worldview that honors Him, and aggressive in terms of completing this task.

Fear God

> Here is my final conclusion: Fear God and obey his commands, for this is
> the duty of every person. God will judge us for everything we do, including
> every secret thing, whether good or bad. (Ecclesiastes 12:13–14)

Our life choices boil down to just a very few significant behaviors.
Solomon concludes his study of the human condition, the meaning of
life, and the nature and mind of God with the conclusion that we must
completely respect God and obey Him fully. All else is peripheral.

Trust God Alone

> Trust in the LORD with all your heart; do not depend on your own under-
> standing. Seek his will in all you do, and he will direct your paths. Don't
> be impressed with your own wisdom. Instead, fear the LORD and turn
> your back on evil. (Proverbs 3:5–7)

The ball is in our court. He has given us the tools and the opportunity; we must take the initiative and actively follow His guidance. Until
we learn that we cannot do this on our own, and that it is His will and
direction alone that enable us to be successful, we will be the victims of
our own arrogance. These passages make crystal clear that what we think,
how we think, and what we do in response to what we think matters to
God. Therefore it should matter to us as well.

THINKING LIKE JESUS HAS ITS BENEFITS

The Bible promises that this quest for truth and wholeness will provide us
with an amazing parcel of riches. Of course, it is not appropriate to adopt
a worldview simply because it produces positive outcomes. No, living
consistently with His principles is the right thing to do. Its rightness is
not because of the outcomes; the outcomes are because of its rightness.

With that caveat in mind, consider the range of the benefits emerging from thinking and living like Jesus. We are promised physical gain, emotional benefits, superior decision-making capacity, relational advantages, lifestyle enhancements, and spiritual health. The more we devote ourselves to emulating the thought and behavioral patterns of Jesus, the more God is able to bless us and use us for His purposes.

This seems like a can't-lose proposition, but remember that nothing of value comes without a price. Even though it is a loving God who wants to shower these benefits upon us, He also informs us that they are not received unless we make a total-person commitment, an all-out, no-holds-barred effort to seek, know, and follow God's wisdom. Developing a view of life that honors God goes beyond memorizing a few Bible verses, attending some church services, and giving a few dollars to the poor.

The Benefits of Thinking Like Jesus[15]

Physical Benefits	Attitudinal/ Emotional Benefits	Decision-making Benefits	Relational Benefits	Spiritual Benefits	Lifestyle Benefits
protection	joy	wisdom	human acceptance	God's approval	success
long life	fulfillment	good plans	honor	heavenly rewards	wealth
vitality	happiness	direction	good reputation	forgiveness	blessings
sound sleep	no fear	discretion	respect	mercy	abundant life
	self-control	insight	justice		

I suppose you could even count the absence of some pretty serious hardships as a benefit of thinking and living like Jesus, too. God speaks unequivocally about living according to the ways of the world, rather than in concert with His principles. In the initial eight chapters of Proverbs we discover that living in opposition to those principles brings undesirable outcomes. Those outcomes make up quite a list: disaster, terror, corruption, premature death, discouragement, the curse of the Lord, mockery, shame, bitterness, dishonor, material losses, physical disability, God's punishment, and ruin. What a stiff penalty to pay for unnecessarily but consciously opposing God!

Jesus drove a similar point home among His followers. Among the outcomes He promised as a result of living for the self are unanswered prayer, unrecognized generosity, harsh judgment, nagging guilt, lack of comprehension, distorted perception, defilement, anxiety and stress, physical and emotional suffering, and confusion. For believers, these will be God's means of discipline; for nonbelievers, these will reflect the initial components of a more enduring punishment.

Let's push the envelope even further. Possessing a genuinely biblical worldview is the flip side of your decision to trust Jesus Christ for your salvation. In other words, if you are a devoted disciple of Jesus Christ, while you were still in total bondage to sin you invited Jesus to rescue you from permanent condemnation by, and separation from, God. Through His death on the cross and return to the throne of Heaven, He made that possible. But in return, He enables and expects you to become a new person—born again in spirit, but also renewed in the flesh as evidenced by voluntary surrender to His Holy Spirit and a changed lifestyle.

But how can you manifest such devotion? By changing your view of reality—that is, by turning in the world's lenses and exchanging them for the Lord's lenses, the spectacles of life. Instead of seeing the world and interpreting reality through the eyes of the world, the change in your spirit now enables you to see reality through His eyes, truly hear the profound wisdom in His words, and personally respond in a more robust way. Your spiritual renewal triggers a whole-life renewal as you progressively understand reality more clearly and live in humble and passionate accordance with His ways.

THE COST OF THINKING LIKE JESUS

God will always bless you when you devote yourself to carrying out His truths.[16] But living in harmony with a biblical view of life also brings some unique challenges and hardships to the fore. Jesus discussed this reality with His followers, wanting them (and us) to understand that a biblical worldview does not make life easy; it makes our lives pleasing to God and personally rewarding. A life of obedience to God will not be understood or appreciated by a selfish and sinful world. Jesus warned people that obedience to God would bring on rifts with family and friends, financial struggles, public ridicule, legal hassles, death threats, imprisonment, physical attacks, unemployment, misunderstandings, and serious illness.

Those who commit themselves to living in full obedience to God will also be more prominently involved in the spiritual battle for their soul. Intentionally and boldly living for God positions you as a prime target for spiritual attacks because Satan recognizes such people as a serious threat to his objectives. God promises to protect you, but tough times will result from your choice: You up the ante once you choose to think and live like Jesus. If you have any doubts about this, simply consider what Jesus Himself endured.

THE FREEDOM TO CHOOSE

So the choice is yours. God will not force you to move in one direction or the other; it is completely up to you. That's the nature of free will: There are right and wrong choices, but He leaves the selection in your hands. Every choice creates consequences, of course, and choosing to think like Jesus or think in some other manner is no different. Bear in mind that the route you embrace—faith and obedience, cheap grace, self-interest, or blatant rejection of God's ways—will determine the nature of and fulfillment achieved from your earthly and post-death experience.

The most important decision you will ever make is how to respond to Jesus Christ's death and resurrection in relation to your own mortality. The second most important decision you will make relates to how you will live in light of your first decision.

If you have not accepted Jesus as the total Lord and Master of your life, go no further in this book until you come to a conclusion on that matter. Talk to dedicated followers of Jesus about the reasons for their decision to embrace Him. Read what the Bible has to say on the issue.[17] Pray to God, even if you're not sure you believe in Him, and ask for wisdom and direction. Consult other books that examine the issues of sin, forgiveness, grace, and eternal salvation in greater detail. Do not allow your fate to be determined by default.[18] Make an intentional and informed choice and pursue it to its logical end.

Perhaps you have accepted Jesus as your only hope, but realize that you have not yet figured out how to live in the fullness of that choice by knowing and observing God's principles and commands every waking moment of your life. That is, you have the acceptance of God but not the mind and heart of God. Then join me on a journey as we attempt to learn how to think like Jesus so that we may live more like Him. It promises to be quite a ride.

Two

The American State of Mind

If you have a heart, a mind, and a soul—and you do—then you also have a worldview. Remember, your worldview is the product of all the information, ideas, and experiences you absorb to form the values, morals, and beliefs that you possess. But few people spend much time, if any, consciously examining their life lens, even though it largely defines who they are and how they behave.

For the past two decades, I have been conducting national surveys to track key aspects of people's worldviews. Let me share some of what I've discovered about the worldview elements of born-again Christians.[1]

Why examine the life lens of only that group of people? Because they represent the foundation of God's Church and are the very people on whom He relies to communicate His principles and standards to others. If the born-again constituency has a life lens that accurately represents God's view of reality, then there is a firm foundation on which to build the Church and a culture that understands, loves, fears, serves, honors, and glorifies God. But if the born-again community generally does not possess a worldview that squares with Scripture, then we have a much bigger and more serious problem to address.

POSSESSING A BIBLICAL WORLDVIEW

To ascertain the nature of people's worldview, we ask how they make their moral and ethical choices. After extensive interviewing of a large

19

cross section of the nation's population, we have learned that there are several popular perspectives that drive people's moral decision making.

Among born-again adults,

- Six out of ten follow a set of specific principles or standards they believe in that serve as behavioral guidelines.

- Two out of ten born-again adults do whatever feels right or comfortable in a given situation.

- One out of ten born-again individuals do whatever they believe will make the most people happy or will create the least amount of conflict with others.

- About one out of ten believers make their moral choices on the basis of whatever they think will produce the most personally beneficial outcome, whatever they believe their family or friends would expect them to do, or whatever they think other people would do in the same situation.

Moral Absolutes

Among the largest group—those who say they base their moral decisions on specific principles and standards—we then ask about the nature of those guidelines. Through this line of questioning we discover that slightly fewer than half use the Bible as their source of life lens principles and standards. About two out of ten lean on the values and views taught to them by their parents, and a similar proportion say other religious teaching or ideas shape their moral decisions. One out of ten say the principles of impact are based on feelings, and about one in sixteen say their life experiences determine their morals and ethics. Just 2 percent say laws and public policies dictate their moral choices.

If we put all of these figures together we arrive at an understanding of how people determine right from wrong in order to make moral choices.

Among all born-again adults about one-quarter make their moral and ethical choices on the basis of the Bible. One out of five base their choices on whatever feels right. One out of twelve rely on what parents taught in terms of values and principles. Another one out of ten born-again adults do whatever will minimize conflict, while lesser proportions of the group trust various other approaches.

In essence, this tells us that three out of four born-again Christians overlook the Bible as their shaping worldview influence. But this also raises the question of what the one out of four who supposedly trust the Bible as their moral guide believe that God's Word says about the nature of moral truth. To measure that, we ask people if they believe moral truth is relative to the situation or if it is absolute and unchanging.

If we accept the idea that the Bible conveys God's timeless and unchanging truths, then the survey results are nothing less than shocking.

Among those who say they rely on biblical standards and principles as their compass for moral decision making, only half believe that all moral truth is absolute. The rest either believe that moral decisions must be made on the basis of the individual's perceptions and the specific situation, or they haven't really thought about whether truth is relative or absolute.

That means the bottom line is that only 14 percent of born-again adults—in other words, about one out of every seven born-again adults—rely on the Bible as their moral compass *and* believe that moral truth is absolute. While these perspectives are not, in themselves, the totality of a Bible-based worldview, they form the foundation on which such a life lens is based. Very few born-again Christians have the foundation in place.

For the sake of context, if we examine how many other adults—that is, people who are not born-again Christians—maintain a biblical worldview, the numbers are anemic. For instance, just 2 percent of those who attend a Christian church but are not born again (a segment that represents about half of the church-going population) have the foundation of a biblical worldview in place. Among adults associated with a Protestant church, 9 percent have a biblical life lens foundation, compared to 1 percent among Catholics.

There are huge generational differences as well. While 7 percent of those in the Builder and Seniors generations (those in their late fifties or older) base their moral decisions on the Bible and contend that morality is absolute, and 10 percent of the Baby Boomers concur, just 3 percent of the Baby Busters and only 4 percent of the oldest quarter of the Mosaic generation have a similar perspective.[2] Not surprisingly, women are nearly twice as likely as men to base their moral decisions on the Bible and say that morality is based on absolutes (7 percent versus 4 percent, respectively).

Overall, just 6 percent of American adults possess a solid foundation on which to build a biblical worldview.

Spiritual Beliefs

But your view of life is not based solely on your perception of moral absolutes. Religious beliefs also play a central role in people's understanding and response to life. If we want to know whether people think like Jesus we must examine their core spiritual beliefs too.

For years we have used a standard battery of six questions that begin to reveal people's adoption of central biblical principles. Specifically, we examine the following beliefs:

- God is the all-knowing, all-powerful Creator of the universe who still rules that universe today.
- When Jesus Christ was on earth He lived a sinless life.
- Satan is not just a symbol of evil but is a real, living entity.
- A person cannot earn his or her eternal salvation by being good or doing good things for other people; that salvation is the free gift of God.

- Every person who believes in Jesus Christ has a personal responsibility to share his or her faith in Him with other people who believe differently.
- The Bible is totally accurate in all that it teaches.

These six statements are, of course, an incomplete inventory of a person's belief system. There are many additional elements that we would ideally include in a full profile of someone's spiritual perspective. To more completely think like Jesus we would have to consider views on worship, love, obedience, stewardship, service to the needy, accountability, forgiveness, and so forth.

Using even this limited scope of indicators, however, we find something very disturbing. Let's say we define a biblical worldview as one in which a person believes that the Bible is the moral standard, believes that absolute moral truths exist and are conveyed through the Bible, and the person possesses an appropriate point of view regarding each of the six belief statements listed above. By that definition we discover that only 9 percent of born-again adults have a biblical worldview! Another 6 percent believe in absolute moral truth and that the Bible is the repository of that truth, but they do not hold appropriate views on the six theological statements. And, of course, the most disturbing finding of all is that 85 percent of America's born-again adults do not possess either the foundation or the beliefs to qualify as having a biblical worldview.

Let me restate this in a different form: Ninety-one percent of all born-again adults do not have a biblical worldview; 98 percent of all born-again teenagers do not have a biblical worldview.

If your heart did not just drop to the floor, you don't understand the implications of these chilling facts. When people wonder why the Christian Church is losing influence in American society—which seven out of ten American adults currently contend—the reason is that so very few think like Jesus.

Let's put this in perspective. As of 2003, the United States has about 210 million adults. About 175 million of them claim to be Christian. About 80 million are born-again Christians. Roughly 7 million have a biblical worldview. That is just one out of every 30 adults in this nation.

God does not need a majority to get His will accomplished in our world. But these figures give new meaning to the biblical description of true believers as "the remnant."

ARE THOSE WHO THINK LIKE JESUS DIFFERENT?

It is instructive to examine the lifestyle of those who possess a biblical view of reality to determine if that worldview makes any real difference in their life. Does thinking like Jesus represent the *transforming of your mind* as referred to in the Bible?

The survey data showed some remarkable distinctions when we compared three different types of measures—daily activity, religious activity, and religious beliefs—among three segments of people: those who have a biblical worldview, those who are born again but do not have a biblical worldview, and individuals who are not born again.

Daily Activity

For instance, Christians who have a biblical worldview are nine times more likely than all other people to avoid adult-only material on the Internet; four times more likely than other believers to boycott objectionable companies or products; almost four times as likely as nonbelievers and twice as likely as other believers to pray for the president of the United States during the week and to intentionally not view a movie or video specifically because of its objectionable content; and twice as likely as other adults to volunteer time to help needy people. They are also more likely than other adults to go out of their way to offer encouraging words to people who are discouraged, and they're several times less likely to use tobacco products.

Religious Activity

The differences are no less significant regarding religious activity. In a typical week, believers who have a biblical worldview are nearly twice as likely to read the Bible as are other believers. They are also more likely than other believers to attend church services or a Sunday school class and to volunteer at church. They are slightly more likely to pray to God and slightly less likely to be involved in a small group. The differences between them and people who are not born again are like night and day.

Religious Beliefs

The religious beliefs of the three segments of people are also hugely divergent. Here are some of the most noticeable gaps. Those who think like Jesus are twice as likely as born-again adults without a biblical worldview to embrace the notion of having a personal responsibility to evangelize. They are five times more likely to adopt the view that people are born with a sin nature.

Those who think like Jesus are three times more likely than born-again adults without a biblical worldview to reject the idea that the Bible, the Koran, and the Book of Mormon contain the same basic truths. The same ratio rejects the notion that truth can only be discovered through logic, reason, and experience, and that of earning eternal salvation through good works. They are three times more likely to reject the idea that praying to deceased saints can have a positive effect on your life. They are more than twice as likely to believe that spiritual forces such as demons can influence a person's life. They are twice as likely to contend that the Bible specifically rejects homosexuality and to reject the idea that Jesus sinned while on earth.

What the Data Indicates

What conclusions can we draw about the influence on a person's life of thinking like Jesus? An abundance of evidence suggests that having a biblical worldview has a dramatic effect on your behavior, perceptions, and beliefs. Once you see the world through God's eyes, your mind and heart become so transformed that you "automatically" respond to every situation differently

A second realization is that having a biblical worldview makes a more dramatic difference in your life than does simply embracing Jesus Christ as your savior. That's a controversial statement unless you take a moment to understand what I mean. I am not saying that people's lives are unaffected when they accept Christ as their Savior or that such a decision is of secondary importance. If the decision to commit your life to Christ is genuine, then your eternal fate has been radically altered. That decision to trust Jesus Christ alone for salvation is the single most important choice a person will make in this life, and is the starting point of a true relationship with the living God.

But the data shown in the following tables, along with the tracking research we have been conducting for the past two decades, goes even further.[3] It seems that millions of people who accept Jesus as their Savior never really accept Him as their *Lord*—that is, they gladly accept His offer of eternal salvation and confess their sins and profess Him to be their Savior in order to gain God's acceptance and escape the wrath of His judgment for our sins. But their spiritual development does not go much beyond the acceptance of the offer of salvation: They do not continually invest in life transformation to become a more viable reflection of who Jesus is as He lives in their heart and seeks to influence who they become and how they manifest their commitment to God.

The consequence is that millions of—the data even suggests most—born-again Christians have not surrendered their life fully, and thus they keep one foot firmly planted in this world and one foot gingerly lodged in the next. That causes many people who call Jesus their Savior to live in ways that are not distinguishable from the ways of people who do not name Jesus as their Savior.

My point is that when we compare two groups of born-again Christians—those who possess a biblical worldview and those who do not—we find a bigger difference between those two groups than is evident between the believers who lack a biblical worldview and those who are not born again. Stated differently, it may be that the people who experience genuine, revolutionary spiritual transformation are not those who merely ask Jesus to save them from eternal suffering. Instead they seek eternal peace with God and embrace a life lens that enables them to think and thus act like Jesus.

A final conclusion that these statistics lead us to is an appreciation for why the Christian Church is having such limited discernible impact on American culture. It seems that Christians are more affected by society than society is affected by Christians. Why is that? Perhaps because more than nine out of every ten born-again Christians fail to think like Jesus; they think like the rest of the world, so they naturally behave like the citizens of this world, too. They are not the salt and light that Jesus commands us to be because they lack the personal commitment and depth of faith that makes them truly changed, God-driven beings.

THE IMPACT OF THINKING LIKE JESUS

In September of 2002, the Barna Research Group of Ventura, California, conducted a survey based on a random sampling of 630 adults throughout the forty-eight continental states. The purpose of this survey was to look at the impact of a biblical worldview upon Christians in comparison to other Christians who did not possess a biblical worldview. Further, the survey compared these two groups of Christians to the attitudes of those who were not born-again Christians. The results of the survey are summarized in the table located on the following pages.

Abbreviation: *BWV stands for Biblical Worldview*

Key: *"Born-again Christian, with BWV"* includes people who believe in absolute moral truth; make their moral choices by following a set of specific principles or standards based on the Bible; trust Christ for their salvation; and reflect a biblical perspective on six key faith issues (salvation, trust in the Bible, personal responsibility to evangelize, Satan's existence, Jesus' sinless life, and the nature of God).

"Born-again Christian, without BWV" includes people who have made a personal commitment to Jesus Christ that is important in their life and believe they will go to Heaven because they have confessed their sins and accepted Jesus Christ as their Savior, but they do not believe in absolute moral truth, or make their moral choices by following a set of specific principles or standards based on the Bible, or do not possess a biblical stand on the six belief statements regarding salvation, trust in the Bible, personal responsibility to evangelize, Satan's existence, Jesus' sinless life, and the nature of God.

"Not a born-again Christian" includes all adults who have not made a personal commitment to Jesus Christ that is important in their life and or who do not believe they will go to Heaven solely because they have confessed their sins and accepted Jesus Christ as their Savior.

| | BORN-AGAIN CHRISTIAN | | NOT A |
| | *with* | *without* | BORN-AGAIN |
Behavior, last seven days	*BWV*	*BWV*	CHRISTIAN
Intentionally did not buy a product or brand because of boycotting the company producing it.	28%	7%	11%
Volunteered more than an hour ot time to assist an organization in serving needy people.	49	29	22
Smoked a cigarette or cigar.	7	22	37
Chose *not* to watch a particular movie or video only because the rating indicated it contained objectionable material.	50	27	14
Viewed adult-only graphics or visual content on the Internet.	•	9	9
Prayed for the President.	90	82	73

Religious activity, past seven days			
Read from the Bible, not including during a visit to a church or synagogue.	93%	54%	24%

| Religious Activity, past seven days (cont'd) | BORN-AGAIN CHRISTIAN | | NOT A |
	with BWV	*without* BWV	BORN-AGAIN CHRISTIAN
Attended a church service, not including a special event such as a wedding or funeral	79	60	29
Volunteered free time to help a church.	51	33	11
Prayed to God.	100	93	69
Attended a Sunday school class at church.	51	33	11
Participated in a small group that meets regularly for Bible study, prayer, or Christian fellowship, not including a Sunday school or 12-step group.	23	27	12

Religious beliefs

God is the all-powerful, all-knowing, perfect Creator of the universe who rules the world today.	100%	87%	52%
The Bible is totally accurate in all of its teachings.	100	59	25
You have a personal responsibility to tell other people your religious beliefs.	100	51	21
Your religious faith is very important in your life.	100	84	54
The devil/Satan is a living being, not just a symbol of evil.	100	22	13
A person who is generally good, or does enough good things for others during his or her life, cannot earn a place in Heaven.	100	39	16
While on earth, Jesus Christ did not commit sins.	100	51	27
The Bible can be correctly interpreted by people who have not had years of intense training in theology.	89	58	50

Religious beliefs, cont'd	BORN-AGAIN CHRISTIAN		NOT A BORN-AGAIN CHRISTIAN
	with BWV	*without* BWV	
Praying to deceased saints does not affect your life.	76	29	20
When people are born, they are neither good nor evil; they make a choice between the two as they mature (disagree).	56	14	10
God is one being in three separate and equal persons—God the Father, Jesus Christ the Son, and the Holy Spirit.	100	84	55
Every person has a soul that will live forever, either in God's presence or absence.	93	75	52
The Bible, the Koran, and the Book of Mormon are not just different expressions of the same spiritual truths.	85	30	13
Truth can be discovered only through logic, human reasoning, and personal experience (disagree).	71	25	18
The Bible specifically condemns homosexuality.	92	47	27
It is not possible to communicate with people after they die.	78	43	30
A human being can be under the control of the influence of spiritual forces such as demons.	88	37	17
You have intentionally identified specific values that you work hard to try to consistently follow in your life.	97	75	67

If Not a Biblical Worldview, Then What?

Since everyone has a worldview, if that perspective is not Bible-based, it must draw from some other sources of knowledge and perspective. In fact, philosophers and theologians have identified more than a dozen competing worldviews that Americans have embraced. Most born-again Christians have unwittingly adopted one or a combination of those alternative worldviews.

Even believers who generally follow the guidelines of the Bible have some elements of one or several alternative life lenses buried in their minds. It is the presence of these competing worldviews that confuses believers and causes the disruption between their faith and their lifestyle.

To overcome the negative effects of operating with non-Christian perspectives, let's briefly consider some of the more common alternative worldviews. Upon studying these, I was alarmed at how many elements of these perspectives I had adopted without realizing how incompatible those ideas are with the Christian faith. This absorption of philosophical and theological garbage was the result of my own superficial thinking (which I believe is one of the unfortunate hallmarks of Americans) and my inadequate theological training. Years and years of listening to sermons, attending classes, and participating in Bible study groups had failed to prepare me to filter out the trash and embrace only biblical wisdom. Something—something *radical and intentional*—needed to be done about the state of my worldview.

But before I could eliminate unbiblical perspectives and systems of thinking from my mental vocabulary, I had to identify the elements. After exploring a variety of texts I am clearer on some of the competing world-views and their implications. Perhaps this summary will alert you to points of view that you, too, have unconsciously integrated into your thinking.[4]

Deism: The Absent God

Esteemed thinkers from Voltaire and John Locke to Albert Einstein and Stephen Hawking have presented the views of deists to the world. Deists believe that God exists and created the universe, but that He has since abandoned the world to run its course. God is not in relationship with people, nor does He exert power and authority over the human condition and experience. In other words, He does not really love either His people or the world He created. The world was something that God the Creator designed as a dispassionate architect before moving on to His next creative product. It continues to operate without Him because the universe is a giant, complex machine that was well-designed and is self-maintaining. Miracles do not exist in this creation because there is no miracle maker present to intrude in the life of the created things. In the end, people determine their own destiny because they have been enabled to do so and because of the absence of the Creator.

In the deist worldview, morality and ethics are important to civilization. However, without a known, involved, and pure God as the basis of such concepts, relativism reigns. In this view, there is no sin and there is no evil. Consequently, whatever happens is the way things are supposed to be and the way reality is meant to unfold; thus, whatever is, is right.

Nature takes on exaggerated importance because deists believe God is knowable, to a limited extent, by using human intelligence and analysis to understand Him through what He created. The Bible may provide additional ideas about God, but what matters most is our interpretation of reality and the events described in the Bible rather than any alleged special revelation by God. Thus, nature is the ultimate reflection of the One who created everything and gave it order before exiting that creation, rendering personal experience, intellect, and choices the window through which life is understood.

Naturalism: What You See Is What You Get

Championed by Bertrand Russell, Karl Marx, and many others, this view is encapsulated in the Humanist Manifestos, of which two editions have been developed during the past century. This viewpoint comes in two popular flavors, secular humanism and Marxism. While each has its own distinctives, both agree on most of the central points related to the spiritual and worldly dimensions.

Naturalists contend that God does not exist. Our perceptions of a divine presence are simply a projection of our own experience. There was no Creator of the cosmos, and there are no interventions such as miracles or divine direction: Matter and the universe have just always existed. Everything is essentially a unified machine, with people as elements in that machine that evolved from the existing matter.

History and human life have no purpose. All experiences are based on chance. The choices humans make are driven by survival more than anything else—that is the ultimate story of history, resulting in conflicts that facilitate self-perpetuation. Humans need community and fulfillment, but these ends are often delivered through our work, making us slaves to our vocation.

Humans are intellectually and morally distinct from other elements in the universe, but without a holy creator to serve as a standard, values and ethics are a human fabrication with no basis in reality or objectivity. Thus, naturalists have no emotional, intellectual, or philosophical problem with ethics being situational and inconsistent since there is no ultimate foundation for moral and ethical standards.

Having been left alone to make something of the abandoned world, people seek fulfillment through material comfort, personal dignity, and community. Whatever value exists in that world is thus a human invention. Death is not something to be feared or even pondered since it is merely the transition of human matter into another form. To naturalists, there is no life after death; nor is there Heaven or Hell.

Nihilism: Denial of Existence

This dark perspective on life has been most ably exposited by the likes of Friedrich Nietzsche, Franz Kafka, Samuel Beckett, and Kurt Vonnegut Jr. This worldview suggests that nothing, including God, actually exists.

There is no knowledge, no meaning, and no value. Life as we think we experience it actually has no meaning because it is not as we think we experience it! This is the "anti-world worldview," contending that there is no world that requires an explanation.

In some ways, nihilism is the ultimate extension of the foundations of naturalism: Matter is all that exists, everything happens by chance, and there is no divine power that intervenes from outside the system. People do not have self-consciousness; human reason is baseless. Life is complete emptiness; truth is the absolute denial of everything. There is no spiritual warfare, because there are no spiritual beings, good or evil.

This is undoubtedly one of the most depressing and hopeless world-views existent. That, in itself, does not mean that it is erroneous. It does explain, however, why so many of its proponents literally become insane, suicidal, or lost in fantasy. Because their own existence cannot be, since they deny meaning, value, significance, dignity, and worth, they experience unrelenting, self-imposed intellectual agony and suffering without any hope of salvation from that pit of despair.

Existentialism: Meaningless Reality

Existentialism is also an extension of naturalism and has been most clearly expounded by Jean Paul Sartre and Albert Camus. It contends that life has no ultimate meaning; each person must determine the meaning that he or she wishes to assign to life and then gain fulfillment through that pursuit. This view of life proclaims that life is absurd, partly because we have freedom and ability but operate in a context of chaos and meaninglessness.

To avoid a nihilistic view, then, we make the most of existence by creating our own world of value; because our actions reflect our choices, they are right, by definition. Constant conflict is avoided only because what is best for me is usually best for others, too, and thus results in a world where people's personal choices satisfy personal longings and societal interest simultaneously. Recognition of the absurdity and randomness of existence is what enables one to lead an authentic life, which is a high value. Goodness is living in ways that make life comfortable and interrelated. There is no God because such a deity would not create such a meaningless and hopeless existence, with senseless suffering and daily chaos and randomness.

The distinction between nihilism and existentialism is passion: The nihilist sees a world that is strictly objective in its randomness, while the existentialist believes that people may have passion and compassion in their wrestling match with the continual uselessness of life.

Postmodernism: Hyper-Individualism

This recent adaptation of existentialism with traces of naturalism is difficult to describe because it exists to defy description and categorization. Even proposing postmodernism as a worldview is awkward because it contends that there is no "metanarrative," or grand story, that explains life and reality—and that very denial of a traditional worldview is, in essence, the heart of the postmodernist view. Spawned by behavior rather than concept—that is, developed on the basis of sociology rather than philosophy or theology—postmodernism challenges much but answers little.

Consequently, a postmodernist may choose to believe in God if he wishes to do so but cannot compel anyone else to do so. If it is right for that person, then it becomes part of his unique life story, but he may not impose that unique view on anyone else unless that person freely chooses to incorporate the notion into his or her own life story. It seems clear, however, that whatever god postmoderns embrace cannot be the deity described in the Bible because a foundational tenet of this worldview is that absolute moral truths do not exist—or, if they do, we cannot know them.

Postmoderns believe that we have the ability to use language—a social construct that distorts reality for our purposes—to convey our personal experiences and stories, but that such stories are simply personal truths, not validated, shared truths. Because a person's story is personal, it cannot be challenged, but neither can it extend to society to represent a greater truth or body of meaning than that which it represents to the individual. Because there is no objective reality, no truth, and no grand purpose, language and communication are focused on conveying stories that describe personal experiences as a substitute for truth. Moral behavior is essentially a private matter; desire, emotion, and personal experience become the hallmarks of determining right and wrong.

Lacking any absolutes, and seeing language as a fabrication designed to provide people with power, postmodern adherents are particularly sensitive to authority structures and hierarchies of any type. Theirs is a worldview that promotes hyper-tolerance as one of the highest virtues. The natural and inevitable result of this emphasis on tolerance is fragmentation, decadence (although the experience cannot be described as decadence because there are no moral absolutes), chaos, and radical choice.

The postmodern approach leaves no room for external control, established order, or laws and limitations imposed by others. Culturally, postmodernism supports anarchy—moral, political, emotional, and spiritual—as a true and complete expression of self.

In the midst of such a society, the highest goal of an individual is comfortable survival and self-satisfaction. Life is viewed as a random series of subjective experiences with no ultimate purpose beyond survival—although that survival has no real purpose, either. Greater emphasis is placed upon the process one might engage in than on the purpose or product of one's efforts. This explains the postmodern love affair with technology, for it promotes process and technique rather than product and impact. Feelings replace reason, experience replaces logic, and contradictions replace consistency.

Relationships and connectedness are critical to postmodern existence. Whereas existentialists find meaning through individual experimentation and experience, postmoderns find it solely through group experience. Connection to a group is what enables a person to achieve identity.

Consider this: Postmodernism is the prevailing worldview held by Busters and Mosaics, the two youngest generations of Americans. It is widely taught in public schools, colleges, and universities throughout the nation. Textbooks have adopted a postmodern skew, and contemporary music fuels the postmodern fires.

Pantheism: Impersonal Divinity

While there is a clear albeit shaky link (i.e., a belief in God) between deism and biblical Christianity, and discernible connections between naturalism, nihilism, existentialism, and postmodernism, a distinctly divergent path is represented by those who embrace pantheism. Drawn largely from Eastern religions and philosophy, pantheism comes in various forms and flavors: Zen Buddhism, Hinduism, Transcendental Meditation, and others. The group has many common factors that make this approach to life vastly different than any of the traditional Western points of view. Pantheism is hard to grasp because it plays by utterly different rules and assumptions, and even those are difficult to pin down.

Pantheism asserts that everyone is god. However, in this view, god is an abstract, impersonal concept; god is a grand unity of the universe rather than a spiritual being who is holy, powerful, loving, and creative. A pantheist lives to reach this oneness with the universe, recognizing that everything around him is also part of that oneness, and thus every element in creation has some dimension of god within it. If this seems vague and ambiguous, it is because the pantheist recognizes that language is a human construct that is incapable of capturing the bigness, essence, and uniqueness of such thought.

Because this worldview extols the eternal existence of all matter, creation is not an issue for its adherents. People live within a hierarchy of material and immaterial things, striving to achieve harmony with all things. We all get numerous attempts at this outcome because pantheism believes that people become reincarnated, but your next life is a result of your past experiences and efforts; it is a reflection of the "karma" (your present condition) you created. There is no traditional understanding of morality in this view because there is no basis for right or wrong, but good works occur because karma is affected by what you do. In other words, moral behavior results because the individual will reap benefits for it in some future lifetime.

Pantheism is more concerned about process than product; technique triumphs doctrine, resulting in an emphasis on how you evolve rather than what you do and believe. Technique that works is generally individual, solitary, unique, and internalized. From a Western viewpoint, the object of pantheism is mental numbness; the Eastern interpretation is achievement of peace and harmony with the universe through a dream-like state of nonactivity and oozing into universal oneness. Many roads can lead to a positive outcome in this process, partially because history is seen as meaningless, time is seen as cyclical, and reality is illusory. Nothing matters at the same time that everything matters. If biblical Christianity is about doing what you believe, pantheism is about not doing anything, just being.

New Age: Philosophical Syncretism

New Age is a smorgasbord worldview popularized by writers such as Carl Jung, Aldous Huxley, Robert Heinlein, Carlos Castenada, and Marilyn Ferguson, as well as entertainment notables such as Shirley MacLaine and George Lucas. Like pantheism, it is based largely on Eastern mysticism but also encompasses other traditions. In fact, it draws elements from all of the aforementioned worldviews and others not touched on here.

In New Age thinking, there is no transcendent god and no evil power to oppose a divine power or humanity. The individual is held up as the ultimate authority and is viewed as being already divine. As beings who can transcend the limitations of time, space, morality, and immortality, people constantly evolve to a higher level of consciousness through a series of personal, mystical experiences. En route we may have contact with ancient beings as well as encounter any number of other spiritual beings of varied power, personality, and purpose. The New Age view is quite animistic in nature.

On a daily basis, life is worth living because we can enjoy a multiplicity of experiences, all of which are private and thus cannot be shared, but any of which may be personally revealing and exhilarating and cannot be denigrated or denied by others. People are seen as possessing unlimited potential; that potential is blocked only by our own unwillingness to move beyond our current time, space, and material constraints. New Agers are prone to describing out-of-body experiences, revelations through meditation, preincarnation and reincarnation, and crystalline visions of the past and future.

Morality and truth are always relative and changing because there is no standardized, objective reality—whatever we see, touch, feel, believe, or imagine exists because we recognize it as existent. The consequence is an endless pursuit of individual sensuality, joy, and self-satisfaction that born-again Christians would perceive to be moral anarchy.

Humans are the center point of all reality, according to New Age adherents, involved in a spiritual journey that enables them to experience multiple levels of spiritual maturity. That maturity is largely related to recognizing, experiencing, and facilitating the unity of all matter and experience, thus resulting in a "cosmic consciousness" that eliminates the traditional, logical barriers, contours, and limitations of reality.

New Age people believe in eternity and personal life beyond earthly existence, but they do not limit such experiences to the Christian view of Heaven and Hell. Physical death is merely a different state and experience of consciousness.

Why Thinking Like the World
Is Problematic

Of course I have not provided an exhaustive summary of every worldview that competes with God's truth. Satan, known in Scripture as the father of lies, has been at work deceiving people for thousands of years. Discerning and deciphering the lies and deceptions of the world is not a simple task. Especially when those lies have become ingrained in the symbols, language, ideals, and values of our culture and are constantly propagated by television, movies, music, textbooks, novels, video games, and advertising without limitation. These brief overviews are merely meant to convey a sense of what the competing worldviews would lead people to believe about God, creation, humanity, spiritual authority, morality, and redemption.

Knowing that the common communications vehicles of our culture constantly expose us to these competing views may at least encourage you to pause and consider what you embrace as a worldview, and how—or if—you protect your mind and heart from the invasion of these misleading and untenable philosophies.

I Think, Therefore I Act

Some people may wonder why being sensitive to these worldviews is such a big deal. The reason is that *you become what you believe.*

American Christianity has largely failed since the middle of the twentieth century because Jesus' modern-day disciples do not act like Jesus. They fail to represent Him well not because they are incapable of Christlike behavior or out of an absence of good intentions but because they do not think like Him. You and I may profess to be followers, but remember, the most significant evidence of our loyalty is not what we say but what we do.

Let's take a practical example of how worldviews shape behavior. May I, a married man, have sexual relations with a beautiful woman who is married to another man? The biblical viewpoint would prevent me from even fantasizing about such behavior. God, who made me and for whom I live, has commanded that I respect the woman as more than an object of personal sexual desire; that I respect her sexual responsibility to her husband; that I have sexual relations only with the woman I married and, in God's eyes, with whom I became one; and that I should not grieve God or insult my wife by entertaining fantasies of sexual interludes with someone other than my wife.

A naturalist would encourage the adulterous act since it reflects the defensible fulfillment of my personal desires, which is the ultimate aim of my life.

A nihilist would contend it doesn't really matter since sexual relations are just another meaningless act that has no value and cannot be prohibited on any moral, logical, or spiritual grounds.

An existentialist would allow the relationship as long as it provides personal value and was not assumed to provide any kind of permanent fulfillment or higher meaning.

A postmodernist would say okay because the liaison is an expression of individuality and is done with good intent. As long as the sexual act is based on mutual acceptance and perpetuates my ability to survive with comfort and good feelings, it is a reasonable and commendable endeavor.

New Age proponents would passionately pursue such behavior because it reflects the existence that we have imagined and desired and is therefore good and may enable us to reach another plateau of consciousness.

This is just one of thousands of behavioral instances we could scrutinize. Notice that a biblical worldview is the only one that tells people not to engage in random acts of consensual sex. No wonder the nation's values and morals have become so blurred and contorted in the past several decades! Only a biblical worldview protects people from themselves—and does so on the basis of the alignment of biblical truth, logic, reason, and experience.

Worldview Significance

So, back to the initial question: What difference does your worldview make?

Developing a strong Bible-based foundation from which to think and act is the only reliable safeguard against the complete demise of our culture, the loss of meaning and purpose in life, and the rejection of all that God holds dear and significant. Consider the alternatives: All other worldviews embrace life as a relatively meaningless, no-win existence in which there is no grand purpose or meaning, no transcendent deity who created us and loves us enough to give us guidelines for healthy and significant lives, and who has even greater experiences awaiting His faithful creatures in the future.

Keep in mind that while few Americans currently possess a biblical worldview, most are immersed in daily exercises of covert worldview training via the mass media, public law, public school education, the Internet, and conversations with peers. Only an intentional process designed to develop, integrate, and apply a biblical life lens can protect us from the savage mental and spiritual assault that occurs around us every day. The failure to grasp and live out a biblical worldview can only result in a lifestyle that contradicts God's perfect and eternal moral and spiritual code that was designed to foster our relationship with Him, each other, and the world He entrusted to us.

IS IT TOO LATE TO FIX?

No matter how young or old you may be, regardless of your religious upbringing, and despite your past behavior and beliefs, it is never too late to commit yourself to knowing, loving, and serving God more completely. If you have read this far and are wondering if you are in sync with God's principles and standards for life, turn the page and let me describe the seven key questions we ought to be able to answer on the basis of biblical truth in order to shape our hearts and minds in concert with God's will. This is where the rubber meets the road.

Three

―᠁―

Bridging Faith and Lifestyle

If you're like most followers of Jesus Christ, you probably have few reservations about the need to develop a biblical worldview. After all, you already believe in the Bible, you agree that your life should be radically affected by your faith, and you want to live in ways that please God and make a positive difference in the world.

However, when it comes to living in harmony with a biblical worldview, you're not sure how to do that or what it looks like. You lack something that connects a desire to honor God with a process of decision making based on God's principles. You need a bridge.

Sure, you likely have spent numerous hours reading the Bible and even memorizing verses. You have gleaned elements of truth at the many church services, Sunday school classes, small-group meetings, and other venues you've frequented. You've probably had countless conversations with pastors, missionaries, Christian teachers, or seminary professors and been exposed to Christian media like radio programs and magazines. The pieces are all there: inspiration, intent, intelligence, and information.

But at the end of the day, you realize that having all of the required pieces to construct a solid, useful bridge—the foundation stone, the elements of the superstructure, the ties that bind those elements together—aren't worth a wooden nickel without a blueprint. Without it all you have is a heap of parts, each having some limited value in its own right but not reflecting its true value until it is put in context—that is, when it is used for its ultimate purpose.

And, if you're like the rest of us, you're too embarrassed to admit this to anyone because you think surely, after all this time and after so many faith-oriented experiences, you should have "gotten it" by now.

Well, take a deep breath. Relax. You are wrestling with the same issue that confounds (or should confound) more than eighty million other born-again adults in the United States—and tens of millions more in nations around the world. Fortunately, "we know that God causes everything to work together for the good of those who love God,"[1] so your experiences, education, and frustration have prepared you for this moment of discovery. It is never too late to do what is right. Now is the perfect time for you to craft and carry out the plan that builds the bridge between your desire and your capacity to live in harmony with a Christian life lens.

THE BUILDING BLOCKS

To build the bridge, you'll need a foundation, a superstructure, and the ties that fortify the superstructure. Let's consider these elements one at a time.

The Foundation: the Bible

The foundation is simple: It is the Word of God. As we mentioned earlier in this book, the Bible is God's inspired and accurate instruction book for those of us who wish to be His followers. It contains practical truths, standards, principles, and models for how we may live a righteous and eternally significant life. Its depth and reliability give the bridge the rootedness required for safe passage from an unfocused to a focused existence.

Were it not for the existence of that document, we would be left in the same sorry situation as all other worldviews: arguing with other adherents of the same persuasion about the content of our perspective.

It would be a case of following the one who argues the loudest, or the clearest, or most pleasingly, or most persuasively, or most comprehensively, or—well, there would be no way of telling who is the best proponent to follow because there would be no unerring and indisputable standard of truth and clarity.

The Superstructure: Critical Questions

But a foundation by itself is of no real value unless it gives rise to something; a foundation gains value when it is used as the base of something practical. In our desire to bridge intent and performance, we need a superstructure to overlay our solid foundation.

In the case of learning to think like Jesus, the superstructure is the body of principles elucidated in Scripture. In our construction analogy, if the foundation is the Bible, the superstructure is the handful of critical questions that allow us to make sense of the voluminous information in God's Word. Those questions allow us to organize the Bible's information to make sense—in other words, to construct a plausible, coherent, and consistent worldview. Without the superstructure, all we have is a mass of data—or, to stick with our building analogy, hundreds of valuable construction materials that may or may not fit together to build our desired bridge.

The Connectors: Core Answers

There is no bridge, of course, if all you have is a foundation and the posts that form the superstructure; something must tie these elements together. The connectors, in this case, are the principles, stories, commands, and insights provided in the Bible in answer to our core questions.

We have always had those answers accessible, and you probably already know the content of most of these biblical passages. What we have lacked has been the superstructure that organized the information in such a way as to help us piece together the different joints of the bridge and structural elements.

So there it is, simple as could be—once you have the big picture (in other words, the blueprint) firmly in mind. The elements are all there: a credible source document, some encompassing and probing questions about its content, and satisfying answers to those questions drawn directly from the source document. But we need to define one of those elements in detail: namely, what are the questions?

SEVEN LIFE-CHANGING QUESTIONS

There are literally hundreds of questions we could ask that would help us develop a useful and biblically consistent worldview—or that might create the same kind of ambiguity and confusion that most of us now possess regarding the grand themes of the Bible. It only takes a few pointed questions—seven related but discrete queries—to facilitate a practical and sufficiently comprehensive understanding of God's truths and principles.

Here are the seven questions:

1. Does God exist?
2. What is the character and nature of God?
3. How and why was the world created?
4. What is the nature and purpose of humanity?
5. What happens after we die on earth?
6. What spiritual authorities exist?
7. What is truth?

Let's briefly consider why these particular questions are the minimum spiritual requirement for a reasonable worldview.

There are three crucial parties that must be included in whatever perspective you develop: God, Satan, and humankind. All those actors deserve attention through a specialized inquiry into their role in reality.

The ultimate objective of these questions is to provide us with a clear, comprehensive, and unified understanding of all reality that will enable us to live like genuine Christians, as originally envisioned by God. These questions should take us from the beginning of eternity to its end and touch on everything of significance in between those time-space bookends.[2]

Does God Exist?

The critical questions regarding God have to do with whether or not He exists and, if He does, what is His nature. The matter of God's existence determines whether or not we have to pay attention to a divine being. If God does not exist, then the whole equation changes in terms of truth, morals, values, purpose, behavior, and the afterlife.

What Is the Character and Nature of God?

If we maintain that God does exist, then the issue of His nature and character becomes significant because everything under the authority of that deity must somehow correspond to who He is. In that scenario, His nature and purposes take on ultimate significance for us.

Our own lives provide a helpful analogy. If you are considering the basic conditions, requirements, and direction of your life, the role of your parents—your earthly creators—has a big influence on your thinking. If you do not have identifiable parents (or ones who do not participate in your life), then you are free to determine your own values and life objectives without the input of those who brought you into the world. If you have identifiable parents, then there is an automatic relationship that affects how you perceive and respond to the world. The pace, depth, and character of your maturation will differ in direct response to the nature of investment your parents make into your life.

Similarly, God's creatures will react to Him in light of His level and type of involvement in their existence.

How and Why Was the World Created?

As we saw in chapter 2, there are all types of views regarding creation. This is no trivial matter. Our understanding of what God created and why He did so will inform our view of who He is and how we might understand the purposes of God. Creation views delineate the Christian worldview from that of alternative perspectives.

Your worldview should touch on aspects such as how the universe was created, the power and creativity of God, the purpose of the universe in His grand eternal plan, and His ongoing role in what He has created.

What Is the Nature and Purpose of Humanity?

A central facet of creation, of course, is the existence of humanity. Identifying the innate qualities and self-image of humankind, as well as the meaning and purpose of human life, is a vital dimension of a worldview. How we arrive at our personal attributes and sense of significance is as important as the nature of those elements.

Humans are different from all other beings on earth through their personality, ability to reason, and relationship with the Creator. Our concept of human value will affect decisions regarding our relationships with God, people, and the rest of creation; the substance of our laws and public policies; our perceptions of morality; and the needs and obligations of human beings.

What Happens after We Die on Earth?

Christianity alone contends that God wants an eternal relationship with all people but that there are rules that govern the possibility. Unlike other worldviews, which assert that because life has no eternal meaning then neither does death, Christianity sees life on earth as a precursor to a different future—but a future that matters. Delving into the nature of what happens after we depart from the earth has dramatic consequences for the choices we make while we inhabit the earth.

What Spiritual Authorities Exist?

We have already considered the existence of God, but what about other spiritual beings? Do they exist? What is their nature? What authority do they possess? These matters will certainly affect the human experience, especially in relation to influence, sin, and issues concerning spiritual judgment, reward, and punishment.

What Is Truth?

Pontius Pilate asked the seminal question, "What is truth?" Every worldview has its own spin on this matter, and the answer determines much about our behavior and beliefs. Fundamental insights required to complete our life lens include whether or not right and wrong exist; if so, whether they are absolute or relative in nature; and on what basis such decisions are made.

A MENTAL TRICK

For people who do not traffic in philosophical and theological matters all the time—that is, for most of us—these questions do not naturally come to mind. In fact, for many people with whom I have discussed worldview development, some of these questions had never previously crossed their mind. Because we do not reflect on such matters often or easily, we may need a crutch or mental trick to help us remember the questions. That's not something to be embarrassed about; it's better to have a system that helps us do what is important than to retain a false self-image and neglect important matters for the sake of ego protection.

Often, we trigger our memories through the use of acrostics—that is, a word in which each letter of the word represents another word. Every Sunday, thousands of pastors use acrostics to teach religious principles to their congregants. For instance, some of us were taught that the elements of prayers could be recalled through the acrostic ACTS—Acknowledgment of God's goodness, Confession of our sins, Thanksgiving for the blessings He has given us, and Supplication for the things we desire.

In developing an acrostic for these questions, it is helpful to keep the questions in the order posed above because that provides a logical flow to the development process. One such acrostic, then, might be this: BE AWARE. Here's what the different letters stand for and the core question to which they relate.

Reminder	Refers to	Core Question
B	Being	Does God exist?
E	Essence	What is the essence, or character, of God?
A	Authority	What spiritual forces have specific power and authority?
W	World	How did the world come about?
A	Audience	What is the nature and purpose of humanity?
R	Redemption	What happens after we die on earth?
E	Ethics	How do we know moral truth—i.e., ethics?

Perhaps that expression doesn't work for you, or some of the references are a bit obtuse for your taste. How about this alternative: EARTH'S Redemption. Here is the relationship of those letters to the substance of the core questions.

Reminder	Refers to	Core Question
E	Existence	Does God exist?
A	Attributes	What are the attributes, or characteristics, of God?
R	Reality	How did the universe—i.e., known reality—come about?
T	Truth	How do we know moral truth—i.e., right from wrong?
H	Humanity	What is the nature and purpose of humanity?
S	Spirits	What spiritual forces have specific power and authority?
Redemption		
	Salvation	What happens after we die on earth?

For those who don't like either of those phrases, here's your last chance. This option is a bit more "highbrow," since it uses the Greek word for church: ECCLESIA. If this one is easier for you to use, go for it!

Reminder	Refers to	Core Question
E	*Existence*	Does God exist?
C	*Character*	What is the character, or nature, of God?
C	*Creation*	How did the universe—i.e., creation—happen?
L	*Life*	
E	*Essentials*	What are life's nature and purpose—i.e., its essentials?
S	*Spirits*	What spiritual forces have specific power and authority?
I	*Integrity*	What is the basis of right and wrong—i.e., integrity?
A	*Afterlife*	What happens after life on earth is over?

Perhaps you can come up with a better acrostic than any of these. (Let me know if you do—I'd love to help you pass it on to others.) Or, perhaps, you don't need an acrostic or any other aid to help you recall these core questions. This is a process that you must develop to derive optimal productivity for you, alone. There is no definitively right or wrong way to do this. The end result is what matters; do whatever it takes to develop a life lens that honors God and furthers His kingdom.

THE ANSWERS

Having determined that the Bible is a reliable foundation for a biblical worldview, and that there are seven core questions that may be addressed in order to develop a holistic worldview that honors God, we must then ask the natural follow-up question: What are the answers to the seven questions? That will comprise the substance of the next seven chapters, as we touch on some of the biblical perspectives that provide the building blocks of our bridge.

Part Two

DEVELOPING A
BIBLICAL WORLDVIEW

Four

QUESTION I:

DOES GOD REALLY EXIST?

Your WORLDVIEW hinges on whether or not you believe that God exists. If you do not believe in God, then your worldview is freed from any ties to the nature and purposes of God. Your perspective will fall in line with one of the atheistic worldviews (naturalism, nihilism, existentialism, or postmodernism). If, however, you believe that God does exist, then you must wrestle with what that means for your life.

If you are a Christian, your entire faith depends upon the reliability of the existence of the God whom you claim to be your Creator, Guide, Comforter, and Savior. Like tens of millions of other Americans, I have been taught since preschool that God exists. But on what basis do you and I know if this claim is true? What is the compelling and irrefutable evidence that God lives?

Again, from my earliest training in catechism classes as well as subsequent church teaching and personal reading, I have been told that the Bible proves that God is real. But one of the most interesting discoveries I've made on my journey is that the Scriptures do not present a comprehensive, well-constructed argument regarding His existence. Instead, Scripture seems to assume that any thinking person will recognize His existence. The Bible then focuses on matters implied by His existence, such as God's purpose, commands, and expectations.

If you think about it, it is impossible to *prove* God's existence. That does not negate His existence; it merely acknowledges the fact that we cannot provide irrefutable evidence of a spiritual Being who is timeless, infinite, and invisible. This is not because of any deficiency on God's part; it is due to the fact that we human beings are time-bound, finite, and mortal. By definition, we are incapable of fully comprehending and demonstrating the existence of a deity whose nature is so foreign to our own experience.

But we must keep in mind that while that inability neither proves nor disproves His existence, our mere consideration of and search for a superior Being reflects an innate understanding that there is something greater than us that is responsible for the creation and supervision of known reality. In other words, we intuitively recognize that something or someone must be responsible for what exists today. But I'm getting ahead of the story . . .

Of course, millions of Americans (known as atheists) believe that God does not exist. Millions more (agnostics) say that they do not know (or, in some instances, do not care) if God exists. Many millions more believe in deities other than the God described in Scripture. Most Americans, however, believe to some degree that the God of the Bible exists. As noted in chapter 2, a variety of worldviews have been developed around each of these perspectives.

The most important questions are these: What do you believe about God's existence? Why do you believe that? And what difference does that belief make to how you think and behave?

GOD IS STILL POPULAR

It is still fashionable in America for people to believe in God. What they believe about God—His nature and involvement in the world today—varies. Currently, about nine out of ten adults contend that God exists. The proportion of individuals who say that He is the all-powerful and all-knowing Creator of the universe who is still involved in that creation is less prolific—about two out of three adults describe God in that manner.

The other one-third are divided among three camps: those who say there is no God (about one out of every ten adults), those who have a different understanding of God's nature, and the remaining group who believe that they and all people have divine qualities inherent within them.[1]

Interestingly, young people are only slightly less likely to believe in the biblical God, although their understanding of His nature is less similar to the description the Bible provides of God.

THE CHRISTIAN PERSPECTIVE

Christians believe that God always has, does presently, and always will exist. Why? The dominant reason is that the Bible teaches this perspective, although it is supported by a variety of philosophical arguments as well as conclusions based on tangible evidence. For the most part, our knowledge and confidence regarding the existence of God is based on our faith in God and His words to us. We may buttress that faith with various musings and inferences, but our contention that God is real and that He lives today is an aspect of our trust in the Bible as a reliable source of truth.

Relying upon faith does not diminish the significance of the position that faith leads to. There are many things in life that we accept without question, even though they are founded on faith. Identifying faith as the basis of our assertion that God exists is simply a matter of intellectual honesty. We need not feel the position is diminished because it is faith-based or that the primary documentation we turn to is the Bible. As we will see, the Bible is a more reliable source of knowledge than many of the sources we rely upon every day for an understanding of life.

Keep in mind that the Bible tells us if we begin with faith in Him, then He will reveal Himself in unambiguous ways.[2] He does not want to remain aloof or hidden; as we will discuss in subsequent chapters, He wants a relationship with people, which precludes seclusion and isolation.

Theologians and philosophers have debated the matter of God's existence for centuries and have failed to reach unanimity. But there are various approaches that facilitate confidence in the existence of God. After all, there are four unique ways of considering God's being: through biblical statements, logic and human reasoning, Church tradition, and personal experience.

As Christians we posit that everything we believe about God and reality must be totally consistent with Scripture, as His revealed words to us, but we do not contend that all knowledge must initially or primarily be derived from the Bible. Thus, we may recognize God through elements of God-given logic, or human events, or time-honored insights preserved by the Church and handed down over the course of centuries—all of which simply point to, clarify, or draw our attention to principles found within the Bible.

In addition, there are two fundamental ways in which God is revealed to us: through "special revelation," such as personal communication from God, the physical presence of God, and the recorded words of God; and through "general revelation," which includes nature as well as human existence and experience. Let's consider these viewpoints.

What We Can Perceive: The General Revelation of God

The universe was created by God (a claim we will consider more extensively in a subsequent chapter) and provides tangible evidence of His existence. How do we affirm His existence as a result of what He created? Through Scripture, logic, and experience.

Many of the Psalms allude to the intricacy, the majesty, the complexity, and the sheer awesomeness of the universe. For example, Psalm 19:1 points out that, "The heavens tell of the glory of God. The skies display his marvelous craftsmanship." The apostle Paul's letter to the Romans asserts that people know the truth about God's existence and ways instinctively by the knowledge and sensitivity to the world that He has placed in people's minds and hearts. "From the time the world was created, people have seen the earth and sky and all that God has made. They can clearly see his invisible qualities—his eternal power and divine nature. So they have no excuse whatsoever for not knowing God" (Romans 1:20).

Through human logic we are able to ask ourselves questions about the validity of the scriptural inference that God's existence is undeniable because we can see and experience what He has made. Ultimately, we reason that there is no other logical explanation for the world and its design: The orderliness, complexity, originality, interactivity, continuity, and beauty are too astonishing to have emerged without some intelligent and powerful force intentionally fashioning the result. Even if we could explain away one element to chance, we could not possibly assign the simultaneous and interactive existence of all these elements to chance. Our personal experience with the wonder of that created reality leads to a deeper appreciation and comprehension of His being. The Church has historically upheld His existence by focusing our attention on the universe and its attributes and helping us to recognize the implausibility of all other explanations.

The more data we collect about the world in which we live, the more difficult it becomes to argue against God's existence. As we study our world, for instance, we not only observe the complexity and interrelation of the created mass, but also the fact that our world continues to exist on the strength of adaptations to changes. (Think of the temperature of the atmosphere, the gravitational pull of the celestial bodies, the mix of elements that comprise breathable air, the height of the ocean tides, and so forth.) The adaptive capacity indicates an incredibly complex design that could not occur through random events.

The very existence of humanity begs the question of our origins. As with the universe, we could point out the amazing artistry and complexity of the human mind and body. But the questions must go even beyond those factors to investigate our moral and spiritual capacity and tendencies, as well. If there were no great creative being we would have no compelling reason to pursue truth, right behavior, and service to others. The bottom line is that we have a conscience within us that motivates us to behave differently than would be the norm absent the influence of a moral Creator who imbued us with such qualities.

What God Tells Us about Himself: Special Revelation

For some people, however, recognizing the handiwork of a profoundly creative and powerful being is not enough. (In fact, many refuse to recognize those products as extraordinary works but write them off as explainable in ways that do not require the existence of an omnipotent deity.) Theologically speaking, we may associate that "spiritual blindness" to the effects of sin—that is, willful disobedience and disrespect to a holy and loving God who initiated a relationship with humanity, only to be rejected by those whom He created and pursued. But, because of His good intentions for humankind and His loving nature, God has facilitated the continuation of a relationship with His favorite creation by personally interrupting the human experience to make His presence known.

This second type of revelation, labeled *special revelation* by theologians, represents God's activities designed to provide us with personal access to Him through various means. Nobody is likely to encounter Him through all of these means, but everyone has multiple ports of access that foster intimacy with Him. It is through that highly personal intimacy that every human being has the opportunity to discover God's existence.

What are these mechanisms by which God reveals Himself more personally? They include events in human history that show the hand of God, such as miracles; special words delivered to a targeted audience through prophecies, dreams, and visions; the presence and personal involvement of God in human history through the person of Jesus Christ; and the stories, principles and commands recorded for us in the Bible.

Historical events: During the past four thousand years or so, God has intervened in human history countless times. In some cases, such interventions have attracted international attention or historical notice, resulting in well-known tales of God's presence. Often, these are known as miracles, such as when God struck Egypt with the plagues, Moses parted the Red Sea, the virgin Mary gave birth to Jesus, or the death and resurrection of Jesus Christ.[3]

Perhaps even more captivating are the hundreds or even thousands of miracles that each of us personally experiences. These might include walking away from a serious accident unharmed; being healed of a deadly disease after a group's intense prayer; receiving the resources needed to continue just when it seemed hopeless; and numerous examples that you can identify from your past experience if you devote the time to such reflection.

Often, our tendency is to ignore, minimize, or dismiss such events as chance outcomes or results of the natural order. This, however, is related to the spiritual battle that takes place in and around each of God's disciples, to be discussed in chapter 10. The fact that I am writing this book today is a miracle—not because I am writing a book (although that may qualify!) but because I survived a severe auto accident several years ago while on the way to a speaking engagement. By all rights, I should have died in the wreck that morning. The rental car I was driving was totaled; the car that hit mine plowed directly into the driver's door at about thirty-five or forty miles per hour; my car's airbag jammed and never inflated, allowing my head to fracture the windshield before bouncing off and shattering the driver's-side window. The rescue team had to use the "jaws of life" to extract me from the vehicle in order to get me to the hospital. After the emergency medical team carefully pulled the glass shards out of my face, I was rushed to the hospital. Inexplicably, after a few stitches in my face and a few bandages on some minor scrapes, I was released from the emergency room within a few hours.

One of the nurses commented to me how "lucky" I had been that day. But there is no such element as luck; all things have a purpose in God's world, and His purpose was to grab my attention and then use me for His purposes for an indeterminate amount of time.[4] There is no doubt in my mind, or the mind of several other observers of the wreck, that I was the recipient of a miracle from God—an event that defied the laws of logic and nature in order to fulfill God's grand plan for me and for His kingdom. When God shows up in this manner, you do not doubt His presence—but, you need "ears to hear and eyes to see" the reality of His presence. In retrospect, I can assure you that this unusual event is representative of many hundreds of smaller, less readily recognizable intrusions of God into the "normal" events of my life.

Special words: There are at least three ways in which God speaks to us in direct communication. Probably the most common means of direct communication is the "still, small voice" through which God speaks to us—the unobtrusive, quiet nudging that we often refer to as our conscience. Through that inaudible yet noticeable voice God is able to make Himself known to us.[5] (Whether we choose to listen and respond is a separate issue.)

Sometimes He speaks in an audible voice to individuals during special moments or situations.[6] Such excursions into people's lives are never done for shock effect but are meant to capture the attention of distracted people. Throughout the Bible, we read of instances when God spoke to people from His throne—and people invariably took notice.

Finally, there are times when God communicates to us through dreams and visions. The purpose of these may be to warn or guide us regarding a forthcoming condition; to prompt us to speak out on His behalf, as in a prophecy; or to clarify something over which we have been confused or concerned.[7] It is plausible that we might mistake a "regular" dream for a God-inspired vision, but our inability to discern the difference does not negate the fact that God interacts with people in this manner.

Presence and personal involvement: The pinnacle example, of course, of how God demonstrated His existence was through the earthly ministry of Jesus Christ. Here we see the phenomenal experience of God taking on human form, inhabiting the space created for humans, and interacting with people in ways designed to assist them in successfully understanding and interacting with God and His purposes. The historical event may be doubted by some individuals perhaps because it is such an incredible act of caring on His part as to be almost unbelievable. But it nevertheless happened.

How do we know that Jesus Christ was really God and not just another person who claimed to be divine? There are several possibilities, as described by both the Bible and other historical documents from the era. First, He claimed to be God, and His track record on telling the truth (through prophecies fulfilled and historical events that have been verified) and through His death and resurrection support the veracity of the claim. Second, others who had no prior interest or belief in His divinity were moved to proclaim Him to be God; many of them even suffered a premature and unjust death for that conviction.[8] Third, His ability to do miracles on command differentiates Him from all other people and suggests that there was something supernatural about Him.[9] (We'll discuss Jesus' nature more later.)

The Bible: The Bible itself is a document that has been recorded on God's behalf by writers He chose for that purpose. It contains a variety of literary tactics—narratives, analogies, lists, poetry, motivational speeches, prescriptions, rules, family trees, principles, reports of events, proverbs, and prophecies—designed to provide both knowledge about God but also knowledge of God. This was an intentional act of a deity who wishes to be known by those whom He created, using a format (the written word) that is transcultural, long-lasting and influential.

The Bible reflects the certainty of God's existence through stories of His intervention in the affairs of humankind; His guidance of historical events; the life of Jesus; and the trust that people through the ages have placed on the content of the Scriptures. That trust is partially based upon traditions that stemmed from the personal experiences individuals had with the living God.

DRAWING CONCLUSIONS

After assessing the evidence described, it is possible for someone who does not have a conviction that Jesus Christ is God who came to earth to save people from their own bad choices to conclude that there is a mighty and amazing God who is responsible for all that we see and experience.

The same reasoning capacities that would enable a person to posit an alternative explanation of reality would support the discernment of the truth about God's existence by identifying the relevant facts, objectively analyzing them, and honestly interpreting the information.

But God has made it even easier for us to know of His existence. He has spoken to us in various ways; He has written to us and ensured the survival of those words against outrageous odds; and He has even come to live among us, first through the person of Jesus Christ and subsequently through the presence of His spirit within those who follow Him.

You may find no single factor described above to be fully convincing. You may even choose to deny or reject some of these explanations of God's existence. However, the sum of the various explanations that ring true constitutes an astounding body of evidence through which God has chosen to reveal Himself to us while operating within the framework of His purposes and eternal plan. In the end, your determination regarding His existence is still a matter of faith—but it is certainly not an unfounded, illogical, or ignorant faith.

HOW DOES THIS AFFECT YOUR LIFE?

Let's assume that you accept the existence of the biblical God. You must still address the matter of the significance of that knowledge. What difference should it make to you that there is a transcendent deity who has created the universe and all it contains—including you? How should this knowledge affect the decisions you make today?

I encourage you to think this through for yourself. Unless you want to be a reflection of other people's ideas, which may or may not be true and consistent, you must invest some of your ability to reason in the issue of God's existence. Your worldview must be your take on reality, not the most comfortable or accessible argument that someone else has offered for your consumption.

However, to facilitate your reflections, here are some thoughts and related implications for your consideration and which you may consider as building blocks in your bridge between faith and lifestyle.

Will the Real God Please Stand Up?

If He is God, then you are not. Sometimes we dissect the role of God and parcel out specific responsibilities to interested parties. We think of ourselves as *the god of our own lives,* while reserving the role of *God of the universe* for the one true God. But what would happen if we truly believed that God is the God of all things known and unknown—the supreme deity who controls everything?

In so doing, we would have to admit, of course, that we are the gods of nothing. This has some dramatic implications. First, it insinuates that I am not in control of my life except insofar as He entrusts control to me. But unless He gives me authority, I have none. I am responsible to take direction from Him; He does not need to accept any of my choices or even allow me to make any. Consequently, I should seek direction in my life from Him, rather than make choices as if I were independent of His authority.

Second, I may expect to receive the consequences of my choices even when made within the exercise of His authority. His rules matter; my preferences and expectations do not. If I defy or disobey His laws or parameters, there will undoubtedly be consequences for such actions. These matters are up to Him, not me.

Third, the ultimate purpose of my life is not up to me. As the one who created me, God determines my reason for existence. He may choose to give me the opportunity to determine that, but without that expressed consent to do so, my life exists for His purposes. (We will explore those purposes in the next few chapters as we understand more about His nature, His purposes, and the nature of humanity.)

Protecting Your Best Interests

If God, the superior Being, does exist, then it is also in our best interests to understand more about His nature and purposes so as to enjoy His favor.

There are only three logical responses to God that you may pursue in life. Insofar as you have the freedom to pursue these options, you may choose to live in defiance of His authority; in ignorance of His authority; or in compliance with His authority.

If God is the all-powerful, all-knowing, just and fair presence (as will be argued in the next chapter), then defiance will certainly result in punishment and suffering.[10] Ignoring His commands and expectations would result in the same outcomes as defiance. The only reasonable approach, then, would be to live in compliance with God's ways. That strategy holds the best probability of producing positive life outcomes for us.

What the Process Tells Us

Think about the nature of anything that creates something else. There is always some manner of relationship between the creator and the created object. Parents maintain a strategic bond with their children, hoping to shape them as they grow. An author remains responsible for the content of her story. A chef becomes known by the meals he has prepared. In every walk of existence, living beings who create something keep some type of relationship with and responsibility for what they have created.

This pushes us to consider the nature of God the Creator's relationship with each of us, as His creative products. What is His responsibility in reference to humanity? What is the nature of the relationship that exists, or could exist, or perhaps should exist, between God and people?

To answer such questions, we must dig deeper into the character and purposes of the Creator, just as a child would better understand the reasons for discipline and efforts to develop specific skills by grasping that which directs and motivates his parent. (In the next chapter, we will delve into matters regarding God's essence and how that affects who we are and why we live.)

The Burden Is Ours

Isn't it interesting that One who could create everything around us—obviously a potent and intelligent Being—has intentionally not provided some manner of "irrefutable proof" of His existence, at least in terms of human standards? Doesn't that raise the question of what He's up to in this eternal episode of spiritual hide-and-seek?

Perhaps this is simply a tactic designed to facilitate a meaningful relationship with us. God created everything that exists, including intelligent beings (in other words, humans) with which to have a relationship. But it wouldn't be much of a relationship if He forced us into it. So He waits to see what we will do. If we pursue Him, He is willing—yes, even wanting—to be found and to further reveal Himself to us. If we choose not to pursue Him but to focus on ourselves and relationships with other created entities, He allows that behavior—although, of course, each choice brings with it particular consequences. As we will discover in chapter 7, if our chief aim in life is to truly know God and make Him known, then we should invest time and energy in fostering this Creator-creature relationship by seeking further revelation, wisdom, and involvement.

The very fact that He has gone so far to communicate (if not "prove") His existence indicates that the content of His communiqués is significant. That raises additional questions.

If His messages, conveyed through both indirect as well as direct methods, matter, then how serious are we about capturing those messages, interpreting them, and responding to them? How often do we engage in one-way communications—monologues in which we acknowledge God the communicator and recognize that He has something to say but dismiss the substance of the communication because we have other priorities? How cognizant are we of the fact that when we cease to listen to the One who speaks directly to us that we have ruptured the relationship and invited other consequences as a result of our disinterest in what He has to say? Are we willing to pay the price of such ambivalence with the existent God?

The Frailty of Alternative Worldviews

The initial evidence of His existence reveals that He is not, as the deists would claim, a dispassionate creator who made the universe then disappeared to pursue other endeavors. The appearance on earth of God Himself, as the person Jesus Christ, is tangible evidence not only of God's existence but also of the value He places upon who we are and what we do. The nature of Jesus' tenure on earth reveals that God cares about our existence and wants to participate in our lives. This is not the behavior of a hit-and-run deity. Indeed, the vastness and variety of God's self-revelation, combined with His involvement in our lives, argues against a deity who lost interest in His creation.

In fact, the accumulated evidence of God's existence pretty much rejects the atheistic worldviews of naturalism, nihilism, existentialism, and postmodernism. While each of these systems of belief is appealing in some ways and contains some truth—don't most lies?—none can be considered a useful life lens because all are based on a foundation that says God does not exist. A bad foundation brings on the collapse of the structure built upon that foundation.

TAKING THE NEXT STEP

These are not the only propositions that flow from an understanding that God exists, but they are important perspectives toward laying a strong foundation for a worldview that is authentically Christian. If you conclude that God does exist, then you should address the next logical question in our seven core questions: What is the character and nature of God? That is precisely what we will confront in the next chapter.

Five

QUESTION 2:

WHAT IS THE CHARACTER AND

NATURE OF GOD?

WALK THROUGH THE MATERNITY WARD at a hospital sometime. You don't need to know any of the freshly minted or soon-to-be parents pacing the hallways. Just watch how they respond to the infant to whom they have given birth. There is a sense of wonder, love, and tenderness in the manner and words of those parents. Often they will express how amazing and wonderful that baby is—a new life that they brought into the world.

But there is something much deeper occurring than a mere expression of pride or awe. Seeing the child for the first time ignites or rekindles their sense of responsibility and commitment to the being they brought into the world. Their relationship with the child will greatly determine his or her ability to overcome ignorance and helplessness in order to live a meaningful and fulfilling life. The act of creating something—especially a living being—carries with it responsibilities that cannot be ignored.

The image of a newborn wholly dependent upon its parents is similar to the bond between God and us. Discovering more about the nature of our Creator will help us understand more of the complexities of life in this world and the next.

One of the pivotal verses in Scripture addresses the personal interest God has in our lives. In the Genesis account of creation we discover that God intentionally designed us in His likeness—which means intellectually, morally, and spiritually, not physically—to facilitate the kind of existence and interactivity that would result in a mutually satisfying eternal relationship.[1] Certainly, as the Creator of all things, He could have come up with some other design for us, but He didn't. Because His primary desire was for us to be in a healthy relationship with Him, God imbued us with characteristics that He did not give to any other elements in His creation. This has some pretty significant implications for who we are, why we exist, and how we ought to live.

To accurately perceive the world and our place in it, we must understand more about God. In the previous chapter we established that He exists. Now we need to learn what kind of God He is.

For the answer, again we go to the most comprehensive and reliable source of revelation about Him: the Bible. There are hundreds of passages that provide clues about the nature of the invisible, eternal deity. Those qualities can best be understood by considering them in three categories. We will look at His essence, His greatness, and His goodness.

THE ESSENCE OF GOD

There are two critical dimensions to God's essence. First, realize that He is spiritual in nature.[2] He is real, but in ways we struggle to understand because His being is so distinct from ours. God is not composed of tangible matter, although He has the ability to take on human form, as proven through the life of Jesus Christ (more on that later). He does not conform to the limitations and laws that govern our existence partially because He is a spirit. When we try to understand God, we really can't get a full grip on His reality because it's so unique and outside of our realm of experience.

But make no mistake about it: God is alive. That's the second crucial factor of His essence. The God of Scripture has been, is, and always will be. He affirmed His life through the name He chose as His identity: I AM.[3] He is active in the history of the universe that He created. He is not only the giver of life, He is life.

Throughout the Old Testament we find stories of God and the prophets critiquing the idols of nonbelievers, chastising people for worshiping man-made objects that have no life, power, or character. In fact, the Bible reveals that God is not dependent for life on anything else; He has life through His own empowerment. Again, the very essence of God is so different from our own that we labor to comprehend His being. And yet, again, the fact that He is alive should dramatically affect our worldview.

Why God's Essence Matters

For decades, in the recesses of my mind I knew that God was a living, spirit being. And for those decades, it meant little to me. "Yup, He's different" was about as much clarity as I had on the issue. Based on conversations I've had with people on this matter during the past three years, I know that many others have unconsciously arrived at the same ambiguous conclusion.

What difference does God's spirituality and aliveness make to us? Given the fact that He exists and has created all that exists, His continued presence among us demands that we respond to His existence in some meaningful way. In the same way that you are affected to some measure by everything in your environment, God's existence impacts you too. People or institutions, such as your boss, pastor, small-group leader, teachers, family, police, or federal government influence what you think, say, and do—even if your reactions may become so automatic that you don't even realize you're aligning your life to them. Your response to their influence shapes your life. How you choose to respond to God's existence also directs the nature of your life.

And make no mistake about it: You do respond to God's existence, one way or another—conscious or unconscious—intended or unintended. Every choice you make is impacted by your perception of who God is.

Perhaps this strikes you as strange or even inaccurate. If so, chances are that you recognize you cannot respond to a spirit the same way you respond to your family, your friends, your teachers, or even your pet. Because we live in a world in which the tangible gets our attention, we have to intentionally reorient ourselves to respond meaningfully to the intangible. In other words, we must retrain ourselves to treat someone that we cannot see, hear, or touch just as purposefully as we would respond to someone standing next to us. (This is one reason, for instance, why we have a division in the Christian Church between those who are "charismatic" and those who are not. Both groups believe in God but have different ways of experiencing, understanding, and responding to a living God who becomes present to us through different means than we are used to.)

Consider the situation of an adult who endures a serious accident that results in the sudden loss of sight and hearing. That person continues to live in the same world but must discover new ways of gathering, interpreting, and acting upon information. In like manner, we must learn to filter our life decisions through the lens of God's invisible but real existence.

For many of us, developing this aspect of our life lens is both disorienting and challenging. Paying attention to Someone with whom we cannot communicate in the most common ways seems odd at best, and downright absurd at worst. Yet no matter how uncomfortable we may be with this challenge, the reality remains unchanged: God lives, He seeks to interact with us, and whether or not we exploit that opportunity is up to us, not to Him. He has created us with the capacity to sense His presence, to communicate with Him, to love Him and be loved by Him, and to enjoy our involvement in His life. But all of that requires our action. The ball is in our court.

THE GREATNESS OF GOD

When we think of greatness, we might picture the biggest, the best, the most unusual, the most effective, the most complex in human experience.

We might conjure images of Michael Jordan performing amazing exploits on a basketball court, Wolfgang Mozart writing orchestral masterpieces before reaching adolescence, Billy Graham reaching millions of people all over the world with the gospel of Jesus Christ, Christian Barnard performing the first successful heart transplant, or Mother Teresa forsaking the riches of the world to serve the poorest of the poor.

But even the most phenomenal human accomplishments and capabilities pale in comparison to the greatness of God. Even a cursory examination of the qualities that reflect His greatness shows that we have nothing that is even remotely comparable to His standing. His greatness far surpasses anything to which we have ever been exposed. He literally seems like a comic-book hero—a being with qualities so pure and exaggerated it is difficult for us to relate to Him.

Aspects of His Greatness

Let's consider some core aspects of His greatness related to knowledge, power, presence, and personality.

He knows everything that ever has been or will be. Not to sound facetious, but God literally is the great cosmic know-it-all. That should not be surprising since He created it all and gives it all life and purpose (which we will discuss in the next chapter). The Bible tells us there is nothing that happens that He does not know about, nothing that He cannot see or understand, and nothing that He is unaware of historically, presently, or in the future.[4]

God's complete knowledge is not simply a vast storehouse of information. His knowledge is affected by total wisdom—the intelligence and discernment required to interpret and apply that information in the perfect way. The scope of His insight far exceeds anything we have ever fabricated through the best combination of human effort, science, and technology. God's wisdom is described in Scripture as life-giving, insightful, just, right, eternal, unmatched, and fully possessed only by

Him.[5] It is also accessible to those who seek it and to whom God chooses to give it.[6]

He has unmatched power and authority. God has unfathomable power and authority over all created things. What we call miracles are demonstrations of God's ability to change the laws of reality. He can control the weather, or the nature and destiny of a person's life, with equal ease.[7]

Interestingly, God's power and authority are not unlimited. (To some this idea seems blasphemous, but it stands to reason based on what God has revealed about Himself in the Bible.) For instance, He does not have the power to do things that contradict His nature—say, to sin, since that would contradict His holiness, or to lie, since that would undermine His integrity. Although He is the Lord of history, He cannot change what has already happened. As an eternal being who always was, is, and will be, He cannot die. He cannot cease to be God. But these "limitations" are not disabilities or weaknesses. They merely emphasize the perfection, consistency, reliability, and unity of His character and capabilities.

He is anywhere He wants or needs to be, whenever He so chooses. As creatures limited by time and space, we struggle with the notion that God can be anywhere or even everywhere simultaneously and effortlessly. Yet that is one of the mind-boggling aspects of His nature. Theologians sometimes refer to this as the quality of omnipresence or "infiniteness" —no limits, no boundaries, no parameters to His presence. Unlike us, God can be in multiple places at the same time; this is attributable to His spirit nature and His authority over everything He has created (including time and space). He existed before He created time, and thus He transcends time. He was before there was anything else and thus transcends the tangible universe.[8] Yet, wherever He is present, He does not take up space because He is spiritual, not physical. His presence is astounding: There is no place where we may hide from Him, and there is no time when we are far from Him, yet we never feel claustrophobic in His presence.

He is personal—in fact, He is "tri-personal." The Bible describes God as one Being represented in three unique but indivisible persons. This concept, commonly known as the Trinity, or among theologians as the triune or tri-personal God, again points to the spiritual nature of God: No physical being could be three separate but united entities simultaneously. All three representations of God—known to us as God the Father, God the Son (in other words, Jesus Christ), and God the Holy Spirit—possess all of the natural, moral, and essential attributes of the aggregate spiritual deity we know as God.[9] He is not three distinct gods joined together but one united deity whose fullness can best be understood in three distinct personalities.

This triune Being exhibits personality traits we can identify and relate to. For instance, we can see throughout the Bible that God uses a name He chose for Himself, providing a carefully chosen identity.[10] We read the Scriptures about God interacting directly with people—Adam and Eve, Moses, Noah, Abraham, the prophets, Paul, John—thereby indicating His relational nature. We discover that He has emotions related to His interaction with people, such as anger, jealousy, love, compassion, grief, and hatred.[11] The God of Israel is not merely some disembodied mass of spirit stuff existing in places we cannot penetrate with attributes we cannot comprehend. This God made us in His likeness and retains the qualities required for us to know Him in very personal and intimate ways.

The Trinity is one of those facets of the spiritual world that remains a perplexing mystery for us. We do our best to comprehend this complex nature of God but struggle to make sense of it—not because it may not be real, but due to the intellectual barriers we create.

Why God's Greatness Matters

Being created in the image of God gives us significant clues as to how we may live. Even more than that, the fact that God has given us characteristics that He has adopted for Himself ought to be a point of encouragement to us: We must matter to Him if He chose to grant us a measure of His core characteristics. Possessing those attributes also implies that we have great innate potential.

The realization that God has power, authority, knowledge, wisdom, presence, and personality in greater measure than we can comprehend may also be viewed from the perspective of self-interest. For instance, all of these attributes and their effects are available to us! The truism *You can't give what you do not have* is appropriate here—as is its corollary *(You cannot receive what someone does not have to give)*. After all, He was able to give Solomon amazing wisdom only because He has it to give, and He freely chose to do so. He put rulers in positions of power because it is within His authority to do so. He grants us insight when it pleases Him because He is able to open our minds and hearts to grasp previously unrecognized truths and possibilities. He comes alongside us to comfort or guide us because He knows all and is present anywhere at any moment it suits Him.

His inescapable presence suggests that He is continually aware of our condition and is readily accessible to us—if we choose to avail ourselves of that access. We may also feel secure in the knowledge that whatever He has promised will be fulfilled. He has the power to do what He offers, the knowledge to do it most appropriately, and the presence to deliver it.

Every day we respond to the cues given by leaders—the people who see beyond the moment to a better future, and who act to bring about that superior existence. If we are willing to take direction from those fallible, limited leaders, then consider the leadership capacity of God! He imagines and determines all future outcomes, making Him the quintessential visionary. He monitors and manages all of reality, and nothing occurs without His knowledge and permission, rendering Him the ultimate facilitator of results. Even in our limited human wisdom, then, we can see the intelligence and value in paying Him homage and obeying

His commands. He, alone, is ultimately in control of our lives.

But all of these lessons must be placed within the context of His relational nature. If God wants to interact with us, as seems apparent (see more on this in chapter 7), then we must respond to who He is. Just as we treat people of greatness or stature (presidents or military leaders, for example) with respect, we must do so with God—and even more so! If we recognize the substance of His greatness, it is because He has allowed us to comprehend those qualities (and, in some cases, possess them to some moderate degree). Certainly, a being of His magnitude and nature is worthy of our utmost attention, awe, respect and compliance.

THE GOODNESS OF GOD

How fortunate we are to have a God who did not create us to be His personal toys or puppets. We can understand this better by exploring his moral attributes—the things that portray His goodness. Those factors include His holiness, loving nature, faithfulness, righteousness, and reliability.

Aspects of His Goodness

God is holy. God alone is morally pure—completely devoid of sin and wrong motives.[12] Because behavior springs forth from one's moral essence, His choices and actions are always right, appropriate, and perfect. Because of His single-minded purity, He cannot be tempted by evil. An important example of this is Jesus' unwavering rejection of Satan's best offers.[13] (Keep in mind that Satan's best offers are a joke to God, since everything that Satan controls has been granted to him by God. If God really wanted anything He'd take it, for He has the power and authority to rule over anything He has created. But we mustn't minimize the significance and the genuineness of Satan's temptations. They also prove God's holiness: Without temptations, one cannot sin or be impure. Only through His perfect choices did Jesus demonstrate that God, who is consistent, is always holy.)

God's holiness intimates that He is utterly perfect and virtuous. Technically, the word *holy* means to be "set apart." God is profoundly set apart, different, holy. Indeed, God called us to "be holy because I am holy."[14] That is the model provided by the One who created us in His likeness to imitate that essence. But His holy nature also means that He cannot tolerate the presence of sin or evil—a striking caution concerning our choices.

God always exhibits love. This is certainly one of the best known and most important qualities of God because of its encompassing impact on us. The apostle John, a recipient of Jesus' affection, was inspired to write of the revealed heart of the Lord[15] that "God is love." Because His very nature is love, it is only natural that the Bible so often notes how God loves us: What other impulse would supersede this one, without just cause?

God showed His amazing love for people from the very beginning of human existence—from providing paradise and explaining the ground rules to establishing kings for his errant people and keeping His promises with followers who constantly broke theirs. The defining act of love, however, was when God sent Jesus to earth as a sacrifice for sins for which He was not responsible on behalf of people who did not deserve such love. What greater love can one have than to lay down his life for those who do not deserve such a sacrifice?[16]

In practical terms, we experience God's love in five distinct ways: through His affection, benevolence, forgiveness and acceptance, patience, and gentleness.

First, He shows us unmerited and unrestrained *affection*. He loves us for who we are rather than for what we do. Second, His love is manifested through acts of *benevolence*, such as caring and protection. He is cognizant of our needs and thus looks after our best interests even better than we do, delivering a selfless love. Third, God's love is special because it provides us *forgiveness and acceptance.* This is experienced as both grace and mercy, neither of which we deserve but both of which we desperately require. Fourth, God's *patience* with us represents a form of love through endurance and perseverance when no such understanding may be warranted. Finally, His love is characterized by *gentleness.* It is not forced upon us, nor is it demanding; it is comforting and pleasing.

God is faithful. The fact that He proves to be honest, loyal, and unequivocally reliable is truly a marvel. No wonder David, who had as close a relationship with God as any human we know of, inquired of the Lord, "What are mortals that you should care for us, mere humans that you should care for us?"[17] God's faithfulness is unfailing in its consistency and availability; it is not contingent on our behavior or emotions because it is a stable and inherent quality of God's.

We experience His faithfulness every time He keeps His promises, which He invariably does, regardless of the conditions. We experience His faithfulness through His "stickiness"—that is, He never gives up on us even though we may give up on ourselves. We experience this faithfulness through the trust we can place in Him to do what is right and ultimately most helpful. We are able to rest in the assurance of knowing that if we have established a relationship with Him, He will be a more dependable friend than any we could ever find.

God always is right and does what is right. The Bible indicates that God is righteous.[18] In our culture, the term "righteous" has various connotations—a common negative one makes us think of people who are *self*-righteous. In truth, the only being to ever exist who could justify self-righteousness is God. That is because He is the only being whose nature is characterized by unerringly knowing, desiring, and doing what is absolutely consistent with the laws of the universe.

Righteousness is not just knowing what is proper, but acting on that knowledge. God's omniscience gives Him perfect knowledge of what is right, and He has the power to do what is right, but He must also have the will to blend knowledge and power into action. It is this harmony of wisdom, ability, and behavior that enables the Bible to declare, "The LORD is righteous in everything he does."[19]

God is completely reliable. In the best sense possible, God is predictable in His ways. He reveals Himself sufficiently so that we know who He is and the core of His essence, and He is unchanging in His moral convictions, standards, and responses.[20] Once we discern what He thinks, expects, and does, we can count on that to remain unchanged for the duration of our lives. He is, in other words, perfectly dependable.

God does not change His character or how we experience the essence of that character. He is active in our lives and in the world, but we can know with absolute certainty that His personal nature as well as His hopes for us will never change. As the writer of the letter to the Hebrews famously expressed it, the essential qualities of God are "the same yesterday, today, and forever."[21]

Why God's Goodness Matters

Are you getting a deeper understanding of just how spectacular, unique, and awesome our God is? The simple fact that He, alone, is holy should dramatically affect how we enter into and sustain a relationship with Him. What a privilege it is to know and be known by such a Being! What reverence, fear, and gratitude we ought to have in our interactions with Him. He is a loyal and loving friend, yes, but a friend deserving of and requiring a wholly different approach. He will never be a friend who is merely on our level. As we will see later, we have the ability to connect with God only through the spiritual restoration we receive through the death and resurrection of Jesus Christ and the power to transcend temptation and sin provided to us by the Holy Spirit. God otherwise could not tolerate our sinful tendencies. My observation is that few among us recognize the significance of His holiness.

Indeed, His love cannot be fully experienced without the presence of Jesus Christ in our life. To receive love, we must be lovable. To a holy, true, and just God, we have no grounds for being lovable—until Jesus protects us from God's justice and punishment and provides a means for us to gain God's acceptance and love.

WHY YOU SHOULD CARE

Our discussion here is not just an academic enumeration of God's nature or how we can benefit from Him. God is the role model. We must therefore examine ourselves to determine how we measure up to the One in whose likeness we were created for the purpose of reflecting that image. Do we allow God to work within us to become more and more pure in our thoughts, words, and actions? Are we increasing in and sharing the same brand of multifaceted love that God showers upon us? Do we behave in ways that reflect truth, justice, and reliability?

Knowing these things about God is personally disturbing because it means knowing how far off base I am in my feeble attempts at being a "good person." Can I expect to be perfect and absolutely similar to God? Of course not. But reflecting on His character shakes me up like an earthquake measuring 8.2 on the Richter scale. (Can you tell I'm writing in Southern California?) If I am to be a follower and imitator of God, I will be so completely different than what we see in the world today that I can just about count on being misunderstood by everyone—except, perhaps, other believers who are on a parallel journey of faith and practice. Consequently, I had better get used to receiving my comfort and self-worth from God, not from sources in the world.

As I strive to be a reflection of these godly traits, I must remember that He sets the standards. *Doing better than others is irrelevant.* Storing up and spouting out knowledge is meaningless without personal application. Having the capacity to bless God and other people, but failing to do so, defies the model God has provided. The simple reality that I am capable of blessing God is so mind-boggling—and ought to be so life-changing—that I doubt I fully grasp it. I know I don't fully live it.

But understanding God's character is not simply about making us feel guilty for our weaknesses and inabilities. Grasping His nature should enable us to become better people through our grateful acceptance of His love and an intense commitment to becoming more like this awesome God whom we know, love, and serve. It helps us comprehend the purpose of discipline and suffering, which are means to a better end provided by a deity who is not just rooting for us but is doing every reasonable thing to assist us in our journey of growth.

THE BIG PICTURE

When you are sizing up someone you've met, do you approach your conclusions about the person by collecting data, organizing the facts, analyzing them, and then arriving at a series of interpretations? Probably not as conspicuously as we do when we consider the nature of God! Yet our finite minds buckle at the effort of trying to capture an accurate profile of the Creator. (In fact, we have not exhausted all the attributes of God in this chapter; the Bible identifies many others, but those included here are sufficient to make the point.) Overwhelmed by the richness and magnitude of His being, we identify and categorize His characteristics and interpret them as if they were independent of each other. It's a coping mechanism that helps our limited intelligence make sense of something that is nearly—and, in some instances, is certainly—beyond our capacity to understand.

This piecemeal analysis does not do justice to the magnificence of God. These attributes exist in total interdependence. They reveal and support each other to constitute the grand essence of God. A true portrait of God would simultaneously present the robustness of absolute power and authority, unlimited knowledge, an inescapable but invisible and spaceless presence, pure motives and behavior, endless love, complete integrity, inexhaustible reliability, and unmatched faithfulness. Each of these qualities is interlocked with and organic to the other. Just thinking about it overloads and blows out our mental circuits. Before passing out from the exertion of trying to imagine all of the qualities wrapped up in one unfathomable but indescribably perfect package, we simply conclude, "He's too good to be true."

And that's the point, really. He *is* too good to be true—if we were making Him up. But such a God—your God—does indeed exist. And you are an important element in His existence.

When we use an expression like "too good to be true" we are expressing both a degree of skepticism and hope. We are skeptical that such a wonderful combination exists—but hopeful that, if it does, we can partake of it in some manner. As we have considered the evidence of God's existence and character, it is my desire that any traces of skepticism you harbored about God have been challenged, if not eliminated. Absent such anxieties, it is time to act on your hope that such a deity knows and loves you. The Bible confirms His awareness of and affection for you.

All that's missing is for you to boldly experience intimacy with that incredible God.

Six

QUESTION 3:
HOW AND WHY
WAS THE WORLD CREATED?

WHERE DID EVERYTHING THAT YOU SEE and experience come from? How you answer that and related questions will affect your worldview. Obviously this is an issue of major significance. Your beliefs about the beginning and the sustenance of the physical world affect everything including your understanding of sin, forgiveness, truth and morality, the veracity of the Scriptures, and the purposes and outcomes of humankind.

Not surprisingly, perspectives on this matter span the gamut. Many people have held the traditional interpretation of the Genesis creation account; others have been convinced of Darwinian evolution. Some have suggested that a variety of deities created the known world; others have even believed the universe does not actually exist!

To delve into this matter more fully, let's address three fundamental questions.

First, *how* did the universe come about; that is, who or what was responsible for the emergence of the universe and by what means? Second, why was the universe created? And finally, *what difference* does any of this make to us?

THE ORIGIN OF THE UNIVERSE

Every created thing has a beginning, a time when it is created.[1] The universe in which we live is a created reality. How was it created? By the work of the God who has always existed and has the power to bring it into existence.

How did God create the world? Its appearance was a product of His will, His power, and His words. Read the creation account in the first two chapters of the Bible and marvel at the creative genius behind the conception of the universe.[2] If you can distance yourself from the traditional teachings and interpretations of the episode enough to see it with fresh eyes, you can sense God having fun experimenting with His creative abilities. (Think of the "creative types" you know who are so immersed in their own creative impulses and skill that they come alive with joy and excitement when exercising their gift.)

Just as a potter starts with a formless blob of clay, God started by taking an initial stab at making something of interest. He created the universe. How? He had an idea and willed it into existence—which, of course, He can do because He is God. (Don't try this at home; you'll hurt yourself.) Like any consummate creative person, He stood back and checked out His handiwork—a true *artiste*. I envision Him slightly frowning. A good start, sure, but the earth, in particular, seemed incomplete and uninteresting.

After a bit of reflection—for how long, we'll never know, for He does not operate within our time and space constraints—He spiced up His masterpiece by changing the lighting. What a change, too—night and day, light and dark; as He said, it was good. And, yet, it was missing something. There was too much water. So He separated it, inserting the sky. Interesting. This was also a good choice, He proclaimed.

But why stop there? He threw another twist into the mix, providing land and vegetation. It turned out to be a nice variation. The ideas kept pouring forth, and He had no reason to restrain Himself, so He then introduced more new elements: the sun, the moon, the stars, and other celestial bodies. He was creating the best of both worlds, so to speak—a universe that was not only functional but also aesthetically and mechanically fascinating. After a while God decided to add yet more detail to His work in progress. Fish, birds, and other animals were introduced, providing an endless variety of activities to watch. Element after element, it just kept getting better.

But then, like a master painter seeking that final touch in just the right place on the canvas, He conceived the most brilliant element of all: people. Wanting them to be just right, He fashioned them after Himself and gave them many of the same qualities and abilities (though on a limited scale) that He possessed.

When He finished, He was very pleased with the outcome. God had used His creative powers to develop a massive, intricate, and magnificent universe out of nothing—an act that only He could accomplish—without breaking a sweat. I get the sense that this was not work; this was part of the fun of being God—making miraculous, tantalizing, brilliant things happen then sitting back and enjoying the results. And what a remarkable process: He imagined it, He spoke it, and it happened.[3]

But how do we know this is really what He did? Because the God who can tell no lies told us so. In fact, to make sure we did not miss the point—and its significance—these creative acts are the first things listed in His handbook for humanity (i.e., the Bible). But the creation of the universe is so special that the biblical narrative keeps coming back to it— just as we should regularly return to its implications in the development and application of our worldview.[4] Ultimately, you cannot accurately understand your life without grasping the nature of God's creative abilities, choices, and results.

Skeptics Exist

You undoubtedly know that there are millions of people—maybe you are one of them—who do not accept the fact that God created the universe. The basis of such skepticism varies but most often revolves around the notion of evolution.

Evolution's argument supposes that the first living organism appeared as a simple, single-cell entity and then evolved into increasingly complex organisms through a process known as natural selection. Natural selection is a means through which an organism must survive its natural environment and challenges in order to reproduce, weeding out the weakest of species until only the strongest and most adaptable are left. The evolution theory suggests that the single-cell entity not only evolved in complexity but also somehow mutated beneficial characteristics until a human being had evolved. It is a creative and interesting theory, but one that does not fully connect with available evidence. (For instance, the fossil record does not produce an unbroken evolutionary chain to support the theory.)

Furthermore, there is no reasonable theory to explain what triggered the whole process. Even if the evolution theory were correct, it only addresses the gradual development of living organisms until the appearance of the human being. Evolutionists still have to determine what brought that initial single-cell organism into being: Where did it come from, and what created it? If, as we know, you cannot make something out of nothing, and everything must have a beginning, neither the big bang theory of creation nor the theory of evolution adequately explains how things started and arrived at their current condition.

Of course, these theories have a major flaw from a Christian vantage point: They deny the biblical teaching about the origins of the world and essentially portray God and His Word as deception.

The abiblical arguments ignore a lot of scientific evidence and knowledge. For example, all matter is naturally subject to entropy, which means that over time things lose energy and strength rather than gain momentum, and thus fizzle out rather than prosper. The biblical perspective on this matter is that God not only created the universe but also protects it against such natural processes as He sees fit. Because He cares deeply about what He made—after all, it was created with an eternal purpose in mind—He has ensured the survival of that universe, especially that of the elements within it that are of greatest significance.

Why do so many people struggle to embrace the biblical account of creation and sustenance? To some degree it is because the Bible does not provide a complete and detailed scientific record of the purpose and process of creation. However, the Bible was not intended to be a technical science text. It was designed to satisfy God's purposes—which include our getting to know and appreciate Him. The Bible contains enough information about the creation and sustenance of the universe for us to understand Him better while continual archaeological and anthropological discoveries confirm the biblical account. But remember that there will always be an element of faith involved in our acceptance of what the Bible describes. If the Bible did not call for at least a minimal measure of faith, then our entire relationship with Him would be radically different—and less significant.

Intelligent Design Theory

One of the most exciting ways of understanding the creation process is through *intelligent design theory.* This approach is being developed by an emerging group of scientists—including a large and growing body of nonreligious scientists—who want to address the crux of the debate between "creationists" and "evolutionists." That exchange is not really about making a choice between a scientific or religious explanation for reality. It is about whether the universe exists on the basis of chance or design—that is, the random probability of elements lining up without any guidance to produce the world as it exists, or the development of the universe on the basis of some type of comprehensive, planned, purposeful design process.

Evolutionists would posit that over the course of millions of years of adaptation a natural and progressive developmental process was at work that enabled the elements of life to align themselves to produce the vast array of living species—plant, animal, and human—that exists today.

Intelligent design advocates contend that the more we study and understand the universe, the more we realize that the incredible complexity of the universe could not possibly have happened by chance; there has to be some grand design behind it, and by extension, a designer. Although scientists who support this theory do not posit the necessity of a divine designer as part of their theory, Christians would understand that designer to be God.

People on both sides of the debate agree on many facts related to creation but diverge on matters of interpretation. A critical example relates to the matter of the adaptation a species might undergo.

Both groups agree that most living species can experience some degree of adaptation to environmental forces, but evolutionists typically submit that there is no limit to such variation, thus facilitating the linkage from the single-cell organism to the various and complex entities seen in the world today.

Those who offer the intelligent design explanation argue that there are limits to adaptability. One illustration I've heard used several times in defense of the design argument is that dogs can be bred to produce variations ranging from Chihuahuas to Great Danes, but they cannot be adapted so as to breed cats.[5]

One highly respected scientist-philosopher, Hugh Ross, has put forth one of the most compelling arguments I have encountered in relation to the existence of the universe. Dr. Ross provides numerous examples showing that the order of the universe did not happen by chance. Put all of these improbabilities together, and the result is—well, beyond improbable.

For instance, Dr. Ross notes that if the force of gravity were modified even slightly life on earth would be completely altered because the existence and behavior of all celestial bodies, including the stars and the sun, would be totally realigned. If the speed at which light travels were adjusted to be even slightly faster or slower, then the stars surrounding our planet would be either too bright or too dim, and life as we know it would be changed significantly. If the earth had a barely altered tilt on its axis, the result would be a change in the temperature of the atmosphere—resulting in the inability of animals and humans to inhabit the planet. Even the depth of the earth's crust is singled out as significant, as Dr. Ross indicates that changing that depth would alter the oxygen content in the air and thus snuff out life as we know it.

Add the numerous other factors that scientists have identified as being so delicately balanced to permit life—earthquake frequency, the strength of the planet's magnetic field, the rotation cycles of the earth, the relationship of the earth and moon's gravitation fields—and the resulting probability that random events caused such matters is laughably minute.[6] It would take much greater faith to believe in that theory than in the idea that a divine creator fashioned the universe to His unfathomably perfect specifications.

THE REASON FOR CREATION

Logically, a universe that exists by design but without a purpose does not seem likely. One thing that we discover from reading the Bible from cover to cover is that God is an intelligent Being who has a reason for everything He does or allows. If we embrace the notion that He created the universe, why did He do so? He is self-sufficient, self-sustaining, and omnipotent. Why create the world in which we live?

The Scriptures provide what seems like an incredibly simple explanation: He created the world because He wanted to! But inquiring minds want to know why He wanted to! Again, the Bible supplies a simple insight: God enjoys creating things that relate to Him and appreciate Him for His power, purpose, purity, and perfection. Plants are beautiful, but they cannot accomplish that end. Animals are lovable but limited; they cannot completely accomplish that end. Only people, described as the crowning creation of His universe, can satisfy God's desire to be loved and worshiped.

Notice the difference between what humans do for God and what the rest of His creation supplies. The inanimate objects He created glorify Him through their own magnificence and complexity. Their mere existence is significant because it further reveals His existence and the magnitude of His power and abilities. The mountains, the seas, animals—everything He created before humankind fulfills His will and brings Him pleasure.[7] But it is humans alone who can grasp the incredible sophistication and beauty of the universe and give God meaningful and heartfelt respect, praise, and worship as a result of His handiwork.[8]

WHAT DIFFERENCE UNDERSTANDING CREATION MAKES

Thinking like Jesus demands that we have an unambiguous and stable understanding of the source of everything we experience. His earthly activities emanated from a clear sense of who is in charge and what life on planet earth is to be about. When Jesus discipled His followers, He always brought things back to the level of basic worldview. As He alluded to in the Sermon on the Mount, God knows all, God controls all, and His purposes and will shall be completed.[9] As participants in His plan, we can either acknowledge His sovereignty and work with Him, or we can fight Him and pay the price.

What drove Jesus' ability to live an influential and God-pleasing life on earth? He comprehended the power, the presence, and the purposes of God the Father. As such, Jesus knew that the universe did not just appear; it was created.[10] The universe was not created in a void; it was developed out of a sense of divine purpose. The purpose was to display God's grandness and power and to enable us to enjoy Him and give Him His due: total praise, worship, glory, honor, respect, and love.

Understanding how the universe was created brings into focus the fact that there are no other gods. Did Buddha create the world? Is it attributable to Mohammed? Can we thank any other pretender to the throne for this masterpiece of creativity? The existence and nature of the world underscore the importance of worshiping Him. It also removes any argument for worshiping anything or anybody else; He alone is the astounding Creator of all, worthy of the worship He requires from us. Idolatry in the world that God created is a logical absurdity and spiritual blasphemy.

What Creation Reveals

The intricacy of the universe also provides many clues about God's character—facets that cause and enable us to worship Him more knowledgeably, enjoy Him more completely, spread the news about Him more engagingly, and serve Him more meaningfully. The nature of what He has created illustrates that He is orderly and purposeful. His creativity exceeds even the boundaries of our imagination, yet He is also detailed in ways we have yet to comprehend. What He created *works*—it is practical, complete, integrated, and capable of fulfilling His divine will. In order to develop all of this He is certainly powerful, but His is a controlled and directed power, not wielded for show but used for significant and tangible purposes.

The fact that God remains involved in the activities of the world by guiding, sustaining, and influencing world events so as to see His plan fulfilled sends a message to humankind. Given proof that He continues to care about His creation, we, too, have an obligation to exhibit such care and concern for His universe. Identifying such elements provides a framework of understanding that fosters more intense worship and service. It also enables us to interpret reality through a different lens: Nothing happens by accident, nor is there meaningless activity in His efforts.

Since we are created beings made both in His image and to fulfill His purposes, understanding more about His creation facilitates a more meaningful relationship with Him and more encompassing obedience. What does the creation tell us about His grand purposes? The visceral reaction to His design is amazement and awe—intentionally inspired to motivate us to focus on Him, desire a relationship with Him, and bless Him in any and every way we can because of how phenomenal He is. I have had the opportunity to observe a number of high-profile athletes, musicians, and politicians up close, and I never cease to be amazed at how frenetically people strive to give those "superstars" adulation, unique opportunities, and even material benefits. How much more does God deserve the best and the most robust that we have to offer?

(We take His creation and being for granted—it's so incredible and we have been allowed such access to it that we are virtually anesthetized to its grandeur. Get in the habit of taking a moment here and there, throughout each day, to ponder the astounding elements of the world He designed and brought to pass. Every once in a while, pause to reflect on the genesis of what surrounds us and the continued operation of the world. In those moments of illumination, pause to tell Him how special He is and how grateful you are to have the eyes to see and the ears to hear the elements of His work and to understand the foundation of His eternal purpose. The recognition and the response are gifts we cannot take for granted.)

The more we comprehend His creation, the more respect we must acknowledge is its due. Every morsel of reality is His—He created it, He has a purpose for it, He sustains it, and He loves it. Do you respond to created things in light of what you understand their purpose in God's plan to be? Are you ready to stand before Him and give an explanation of each of your actions in light of His concern for everything He made? Humans may be His crowning creative achievement of this universe, but we are still inferior to and dependent upon Him. What degree of respect and obedience do we give Him?

Creation and Science

Perhaps you wonder about the role of science: Is it inherently hostile to God? Not at all! Science is one of the means through which we are able to figure out the amazing complexities and connections of what God created.

The purpose of science has been distorted by some people to be a means of "proving" the absence or nonexistence of God when in fact proper science can only point out the existence and majesty of God. The results of authentic scientific inquiry, which is allowed by God, will simply provide more reason to glorify God, rather than reasons to dismiss or replace Him. Honest inquiry will reflect Him; only dishonest practices will conclude that God is not responsible for the creation of the world. As Christians, we ought to encourage the contributions that authentic scientific inquiry makes to our lives and to our relationship with God.

One of the outcomes of true scientific method is to reassert that God created the universe from nothing—a feat that is impossible for anyone else. We pride ourselves on our creativity, but we simply rearrange existing materials to create a new combination. The real miracle is in the original creation of those elements. Only God can do that.

As you go about your business today, realize that God has entrusted you with a responsibility to future generations. We are not only the inhabitants of His creation but also the managers of it (as we will discuss in the next chapter). Our responsibility is to use and enjoy what God has made, but also to protect it so that coming generations will experience the same awe and intimacy with Him through His works as we have been privileged to experience.

And do not lose sight of the fact that if we have a responsibility to share the knowledge and love of God and His truths with others—especially the truth about what Jesus Christ did on earth and on the cross for the sake of all people—our understanding and appreciation of God's creation are integral elements in that narrative. Establishing the mind-boggling design of the universe as an example of God's intelligence, power, and purposes should go a long way toward helping the uninitiated to grasp the meaning of life and eternity.

Having established the existence and nature of God and the means and purposes of His creation of the universe leads us to the next logical question on our journey: Why did He bother creating people? In such an idyllic world, filled with peace and beauty, what value could we possibly add to the created order?

Seven

QUESTION 4:

WHAT IS THE NATURE AND
PURPOSE OF HUMANITY?

WHEN MY FAMILY AND I travel around the country to work with churches, we tend to watch more television in our hotel rooms than we do at home. Recently I caught a program on ocean fish. I am one of those people who is fascinated by the idiosyncrasies of the ocean's inhabitants. During this particular program, however, I was dumbstruck by the voice-over. The authoritative narrator was informing viewers that humans have a responsibility to protect the large fish species featured on that program because "all creatures that populate the earth have equal value." All life forms, whether plant, animal, or human, have the same fundamental purposes (identified as reproduction and sustained life) and thus have the same rights and obligations toward each other.

Does that represent the worldview taught in the Bible? To make that determination we must explore the purpose of human life, the nature of humanity, and how God's Church relates to all of this. The first of these will take up the bulk of our discussion in this chapter, for it is the foundation of the other two.

THE PURPOSES OF LIFE

We might understand human life as having five grand purposes. God spelled it out for us in unambiguous terms.

What does the LORD your God require of you? He requires you to fear him, to live according to his will, to love and worship him with all your heart and soul, and to obey the LORD's commands and laws. (Deuteronomy 10:12–13)

We can simplify even further. That command from Deuteronomy can be narrowed to two ultimate challenges: to love God and obey Him.

First, we are called to love God and His people (for He loves us so much He wants us to treat one another in no less a fashion). To do this we must love Him personally and completely, we must worship Him as the expression of that devotion, and we must fear Him because we love Him so dearly that what He thinks about us is all that matters to us.

Second, we must be faithful to the guidelines He has provided to us through His Word as the proof that we truly love Him and have committed ourselves to doing that which we know brings Him pleasure and glory. Obedience is more than just following the letter of the law; it is discerning what God would want—His will for us—and choosing to seek that outcome.

Those two tiny words—*love* and *obey*—pack quite a wallop! Identifying those factors as the keys to life answers the question, "What does He want from us?" but also raises the question, "Why does He want that?" It appears that these behaviors are necessary in order for God to have a solid relationship with us and for us to be able to fully enjoy robust relationships with Him and others.

God's nature is that He *is* love. He desires creatures with which He can meaningfully share and receive such love.[1] Humans were created for just such a purpose: to know God intimately and have a loving relationship with Him. You and I have the privilege of interacting in the most intimate and meaningful ways with God the Father, Jesus the Son, and the Holy Spirit. But what does it really mean to have a relationship with God?

A Genuine Relationship with God

The Bible is the saga of God's undiminished desire to have a relationship with us. The nature of that bond is different from the relationships we experience with people because God Himself is so different. We are to love God through full appreciation for who He is and what He has done by demonstrating passionate affection for Him, by allowing ourselves to be spiritually dependent upon Him, and by exhibiting absolute commitment and loyalty to Him.

Such love is an all-encompassing endeavor that takes a lifetime to understand and master. The magnitude of the challenge is so great that no matter how hard we try, because of our innate penchant for disobeying God we will never completely fulfill it. Thankfully, self-made perfection is not the ultimate goal, for that is beyond our reach. Our dominant motivation is to develop the will to love Him, "with all your heart, all your soul, all your strength, and all your mind."[2] That is a sufficiently staggering objective!

Developing a Desire to Love

Even *this* goal may seem beyond our reach. Yet, keep in mind that God wants us to succeed in such pursuits. Because He truly loves us He does not set us up for failure or require us to do things beyond our capabilities. Developing a wholehearted desire to fully love Him must therefore be possible. But how?

Although the Bible tells us that part of loving God is to have a healthy fear of His all-powerful nature, the apostle John explained that if we truly love God to our highest capacity, we will have no personal fear because "perfect love expels all fear. If we are afraid, it is for fear of judgment, and this shows that his love has not been perfected in us."[3] It is the authority and presence of Jesus in our life that gives us the capacity for such "perfect love." When Moses delivered the Ten Commandments to Israel, his admonition was to "let your fear of Him keep you from sinning!"[4] With the grace extended to us through the sacrifice of Jesus Christ for us, that exhortation can now be understood as "let your *love* of Him keep you from sinning." Once Jesus is truly the master of your life, the biggest challenge is to know God's expectations (according to the Bible), listen to the voice of the Holy Spirit that instructs you in their fulfillment, and rely upon God's power to resist the temptation to do that which displeases Him.

Sometimes we struggle because we think of loving God as an accumulation of behaviors that add up to a superior degree of appreciation. But loving God is not so much something we do as something we become: Loving God is about being a twenty-four-hour, seven-day-a-week suitor of the Lord. Again, God Himself is our role model, as the apostle John reminds us that "God is love." In the same way, because He has invested Himself so heavily and materially within us through Jesus' death and resurrection and the subsequent provision of the indwelling Holy Spirit, we have a superhuman capacity to love Him.

In fact, a vital element in loving God is to have sufficient faith in Him to completely *trust Him*. God Himself is eager for us to grow that trust and provides the means by testing the strength of our trust in Him through the challenges and trials of daily life. Our handling of each obstacle, setback, and victory in life can either be seen as a series of chance events or as a means of deepening our faith and trust in God. It can be difficult to see every situation—conversations, opportunities, conflicts, choices—as intentional building blocks in our relationship with Him. Seeing life through such a lens, however, is a huge step forward. Once we understand that we are engaged in an unending battle for our souls and recognize that God is sovereign and Satan is active in seeking to thwart His sovereignty, we can recognize that there is no such thing as a coincidence. Every incident in life, no matter how minor it seems, has a purpose that relates to the invisible grand scheme that is unfolding around us.

God promised that He will not allow us to endure anything that is beyond our capacity, and that every trial produces a positive outcome for those who are seeking to honor Him. Without sufficient trust to faithfully persevere through all the just and unjust difficulties we face, our love for God will lack the depth that is possible and transforming.[5]

Practical Love

If loving God is to be the single-minded focus of our life, how do we do this? Again, the Bible provides clues through its narratives and through the model that Jesus provided to us. There are a handful of practices that make such love real.

Loving humankind. First, we are called to imitate His example by loving the objects of His love: people. Scripture informs us that we are to be lovers of humankind. The reason we are to love them is not to promote "global peace" or "international unity." It's to honor that which is important to God. Just as we want to be loved and accepted by people, so are we to love and accept them. We do this not merely to protect ourselves from unjust or painful treatment but to embrace and carry out God's desires and ideals.

We miss the boat if we attempt to love people by merely enduring their presence, or by intellectually acknowledging that God commands us to accept them, or even by manufacturing warm feelings toward them. God encourages us to show *genuine love* by blessing others through affirmation and encouragement, by meeting their physical and emotional needs, and by living and working in a faith-driven community.[6] These are not optional behaviors or efforts to be made on an as-convenient basis. They are meant to form the foundation upon which our human experience is built. This may well require us to rethink the goals and priorities we have established for our lives.

Fully loving God requires us to serve Him. This may seem odd, since God is all-powerful and as a spiritual being has no physical needs that we can satisfy. However, much of Jesus' teaching was designed to encourage Christians to take care of the needs of other people, whether those needs were physical, emotional, familial, spiritual, or basic.[7] This relates to what has become known as the "second greatest commandment"—the call to "love your neighbor as yourself"—as a means of being more Christlike.

The apostle Paul expanded on this service concept by exhorting believers in the early church to adopt specific character and behavioral qualities in order to love others through service. A prolific list maker, Paul provided several collections that clarify what love looks like in practice. In his letter to the Colossians, for instance, Paul encouraged us to treat each other with kindness, humility, mercy, gentleness, patience, and forgiveness.[8] In other portions of the New Testament we are exhorted to provide each other with love, forgiveness, submission, and encouragement, and to work together in cooperation.[9] The purpose and nature of these directives remind us that what we do is an outgrowth of our character and beliefs—and that these things matter on a much larger scale than we might assume.

Sharing God's love. A second reflection of true God-love is sharing His love with others, not simply as a means of service but also as a result of our excitement about participating in His life. Sharing His love could be practiced through how we raise our children, how we treat our spouse, how we care for our aged parents, or how thoughtfully and consistently we share the good news about Jesus' life with those who are not devoted to Him. As ambassadors for Christ, we are to seize every opportunity to be Christlike, reflecting His concern and compassion on both a temporal and eternal level.

Truly communicating. A relationship isn't worth much if it does not include honest and frequent communication. We relate to God through prayer and worship. The failure to consistently engage in dialogue weakens the connection with God and hinders our ability to stay close to Him. When we experience a breakdown in communication with God, it is a sign that all is not well with the relationship; when you love somebody and have the opportunity to interact with him or her, you naturally and enthusiastically exploit those opportunities.

We relate to people through our speech and other means of communication in order to educate, encourage, direct, and inform them. The absence of clear and constant communication, whether verbal or written, hints at a rupture or superficiality in the relationship. Effective communication is also about the quality of the interaction, not just the frequency. As the Bible cautions us, we will be held accountable for every word we utter, and we are to use speech that builds people up and never dishonors God or others.[10]

Enjoying the gift of life. Another important component of loving God is to enjoy the life He has given us. This may be the most misunderstood aspect, often emerging as a utilitarian perspective (i.e., "the world is here for my pleasure"). Life is a gift from God, freely given to us, allowing us to make life-shaping, world-altering choices. The Bible indicates that the nature of the choices we make will determine whether we are able to experience a pleasant and fulfilling life. To aid us in the quest, God provides ample advice on how to make beneficial choices. By loving God through the enjoyment of His gift, we experience a more profound sense of fulfillment and meaning.

But how can we enjoy a life that is rife with pain, confusion, and imperfection? By recognizing the possibilities and intentionally seeking the positive outcomes that God identifies. For instance, God encourages us to have fun, within the boundaries of holy living.[11] Far from being a cosmic kill-joy, God wants us to live life to the fullest, just as we get great pleasure out of watching people really enjoy the presents we get them for birthdays and holidays. He even exhorts us to find pleasure through good food and through music.[12]

People are a means to joy, too. Family is designed to provide joy and growth. A healthy relationship with a spouse, the wonders and ecstasy of raising children, and close relationships with relatives enrich our lives.[13] Other personal relationships are capable of delivering great satisfaction, too, and are encouraged by God as a means of experiencing richness in life.[14] We were made to be in relationship, not isolation, and the friendships we develop facilitate that aspect of human fullness.

The environment in which God placed us was created to produce joy, whether through our fascination with the variety of creative and practical elements in the world or through the provision supplied from the land, air, and seas that He created.[15] Within this world we must work, and even though labor is a curse brought on by our rebellion against God, He has redeemed our work. Our vocational effort and productivity, as well as the resulting wealth, are capable of giving us enjoyment, especially when we use that wealth in a generous manner.[16]

Because we experience this life in mortal bodies, the Bible proclaims that we ought to revel in the gift of good physical health that allows us to take advantage of the numerous opportunities God provides.[17] In the end, God asks us to recognize each new day as a renewed gift, prolonging our ability to realize joy and fulfillment.[18] But He also makes clear that to love Him by enjoying His manifold provision demands that we be happy with what we have rather than disappointed over what we do not have. Joy is as much a matter of attitude as it is an outgrowth of experience.[19]

Worshiping God. Perhaps foremost in our effort to love God is to worship Him. The Bible explains that worship is not a one-hour-per-week church event or a routine we practice out of habit but a lifestyle that emanates from a reconditioned heart and mind. For instance, the Ten Commandments lead off with three directives that form the boundaries of loving God: Worship Him, do not worship any other god, and do not make idols that could be worshiped. God boldly proclaims His reasoning: "I, the LORD your God, am a jealous God who will not share your affection with any other god!"[20] He then goes on to equate worshiping false gods with hating Him and cautions that He will punish those who do not worship Him.

When God instructed Moses to lead the Israelites out of Egypt the reason was so that they could worship Him more fully. Six times Moses repeats God's words to Pharaoh: "Let my people go so they can worship me." Worship is so important that you find the people whom God used in world-changing ways and whose lives have withstood the ravages of human history are all described as people who worshiped God. Study the lives of Jacob, Abraham, Joseph, Moses, Joshua, David, Solomon, and the apostles, and the Bible describes their commitment to worship.[21]

This is so paramount to God that He promised to give us the capacity to solely worship Him. Speaking of those who would follow Him, the Lord spoke through the prophet Jeremiah to explain, "I will give them one heart and mind to worship me forever, for their own good and for the good of all their descendants. And I will make an everlasting covenant with them, promising not to stop doing good for them. I will put a desire in their hearts to worship me, and they will never leave me."[22]

Do you get the impression that worship matters—I mean *really* matters—to God? My sense is that worship is *the* deciding factor when it comes to determining the realness of your love for God. In His eyes, you either do or do not wholeheartedly love God. He can deal with a weak prayer life, an unstable family, bad behavior, and the failure to sacrificially serve other people, but He cannot reconcile a refusal to flat-out worship Him.

In His reckoning, worship is the ultimate expression of our love and the one unmistakable indicator of our feelings toward Him. Consequently, there is no middle ground on this issue. The authenticity of your love is proven by the breadth, frequency, and intensity of your worship. Either He is or He is not the sole object of your worship. Either you do or you do not commit yourself to constant prayer, songs, fasting, service, meditation, Scripture reading, and other acts designed to praise and glorify Him. The bottom line is simple: You breathe, eat, drink, speak, think, and move today in order to love and obey Him. Each new moment is another opportunity to worship Him. There is no more significant demonstration of your love than through your worship of the Creator.

The Role of Obedience

If we completely love God, we want to make Him happy. We know that He is perfect and holy, and He exhorts us to be that way not only because it is in our best human interests but also because that enables us to connect with Him more fully and intimately. God has confirmed the importance of obedience in four ways: by stating it in His Word, by giving us the rules and commands we need to live a holy life, by providing a human role model in Jesus Christ, and by sending us the Holy Spirit to provide the power to overcome contradictory impulses and drives.

God's conversations with Moses clarified the fact that obedience is about doing God's will. We can know that will through His Word, through direct revelation, and through the ways in which He has gifted us and placed us in particular situations for service to the kingdom. Every one of us has a different calling, vision, and set of "tools" with which to fulfill His will for our life, but there are several common elements in God's will that affect all of us.

Obedience is critical to God because it is the sign that we truly love Him. Jesus taught this when he instructed His disciples, "If you love me, obey my commandments."[23] The apostle John confirmed that reality when he wrote, "If someone says, 'I belong to God,' but doesn't obey God's commandments, that person is a liar and does not live in the truth. But those who obey God's word really do love him. That is the way to know whether or not we live in him."[24] Such obedience glorifies God and allows us to have a viable relationship with Him.[25]

Living in obedience, however, is not something we can successfully accomplish of our own volition.[26] Even though complete obedience is our responsibility, we are not strong enough to pull it off.[27] We must prepare ourselves to obey by studying the Word for insight into the contours of the law, but only through God's special empowerment, provided in response to our fervent prayer, can we become obedient lovers of God.[28] The desire and power come from God.[29] We may appropriate those, but we are not capable of willing ourselves to obedience. Had that strength existed within humankind, Jesus would not have had to die in payment for our sins.

God promises that our obedience will produce a far superior life experience.[30] He promises to "lavish" His love upon the obedient; to protect them from all the snares of the world; to open the gates of Heaven to them; and to enable them to master those things that oppose God and His will.[31] But remember that we do not seek to obey all of God's commands simply because it provides a better outcome than the alternatives. We are called to obey Him because it is the most complete demonstration of our love for Him, and we seek such obedience because He deserves nothing less. To call oneself a Christian and yet fail to fully seek total obedience is the definition of hypocrisy.

Why Life Purpose Matters

We all respond to the things that matter. Whatever you believe provides meaning and purpose in life motivates you to action. Unless you intentionally and tirelessly strive to see life through God's eyes, you will see it from Satan's vantage point, with predictable but disastrous results.

Grasping a sense of God's purpose for your life enables you to align your priorities with His. Being sensitized to the fact that Satan thirsts for your soul and will go all-out to distort your perspectives and behavior should help you to more clearly see things for what they are: choices in a continuous spiritual battle in which Satan believes that you are still accessible to him if he can just push the right buttons. How close is the evil one to seducing you to play his game?

Evaluate your motivation for everything you do: Is it based on identifiable biblical standards and principles that you consciously identified, or on the basis of a worldly measurement of what produces you with the optimal result? Even when you make choices that you believe will please God, are your decisions based on your feeling that you have to do it to keep God happy (which may be evidence that a rebellious heart still reigns), based on the belief that your choices will benefit you (evidence of a selfish heart), or based solely on a genuine desire to make God happy? If it is your aim to think like Jesus, then you must worry only about pleasing God.

Grasping your purpose in life should reinvigorate your commitment to God. Identifying the true reason for your existence provides new insight into Paul's statement, "While we live, we live to please the Lord. And when we die, we go to be with the Lord. So in life and death, we belong to the Lord."[32] Do you see that your life is all about—and *only* about—God? The more you can purge yourself of you, and replace it with a wholehearted focus on and surrendering of self to God, the more fulfilling your life will be.

Sometimes relationships seem like more of a hindrance than a necessity, but if you think like Jesus, you will see how significant your relationships with God and His followers are to your own purpose and fulfillment on earth. Such wisdom may help you to embrace opportunities to serve God by serving others. It is likely to be that reversal of worldly wisdom that finally enables you to fully enjoy life, despite the challenges, heartaches, and misery through which you wander. To think like Jesus— who said, "For even I, the Son of Man, came here not to be served but to serve others"—you must think of yourself as a servant of all, master of none.[33] And that's a tough, uphill fight in contemporary culture.

THE NATURE OF HUMANITY

Once we understand that God exists, comprehend His amazing and unique nature, recognize the truth of His creation, and come to grips with why He created humanity and the purpose He has for our lives, loving and obeying Him ought to be a no-brainer. But as you and I both know from years of personal experience, continually loving and obeying God is the ultimate challenge.

Why? Because of the spiritual battle for our souls that has introduced sin and evil into the human equation. Possessing free will—that is, the ability to make decisions regarding what to do—we can follow God's way or not, depending on our deepest desires. It is the presence of Satan, wielding his worldly lures in light of his evil desires—that makes obedience so difficult.

Many people whom I have interviewed are perplexed by free will. Why didn't God simply make us do what He wants so that we could enjoy all the good things He has in mind for us? But logically, if He *made* us do what He wants, He'd be forcing us to love Him—and that wouldn't be love at all, would it? He seeks a genuine relationship with us because we want to love Him and are willing to turn our back on the best that the world has to offer in order to receive the best that He has to offer. It must be a choice for it to be meaningful.

The choices we make spring from who we are: Character always determines behavior. What is our natural character like? The Bible speaks to that issue very clearly; its conclusions are readily verified by observation and experience. Influenced by Satan, who desires to drive a wedge between God and us, we become confused, discouraged, dissatisfied, skeptical, and selfish regarding life. Our lives become defined by rebellion against God's ways rather than relentless pursuit of His ways.

Throughout the Old and New Testaments we hear God describing our nature. While instructing Jeremiah on what to say to the Israelites, God's chosen people, He noted that they were stubborn and rebellious, a theme subsequently echoed in the message of other prophets and apostles.[34] He later spoke through Jeremiah again, portraying the human heart as "most deceitful and desperately wicked."[35] In the Psalms, Asaph recounts the history of the people of God, summarizing them as "stubborn, rebellious, and unfaithful, refusing to give their hearts to God."[36] Jesus demonstrated

His greatest anger with the religious people of His day, chastising them for being hypocrites, biblically illiterate, fools, stubborn, and faithless.[37] You get the picture.

The effects of sin have insinuated themselves deep into the essence of humanity. Given a choice of holiness or depravity, our natural inclination is toward the latter. Is there any hope for humankind, sinners that we are? Absolutely!

Of our own strength we cannot change our nature, but the power of God is able and willing to bring about a 180-degree transformation in who we are and how we respond to Him and His creation. Through the power of God's grace we can become people characterized by what the Bible calls the "fruit" of the Spirit: "love, joy, peace, patience, kindness, goodness, faithfulness, gentleness, and self-control."[38] Without the transforming presence of Christ in us, we remain obnoxious, selfish, evil-inclined adversaries of God, whether we think of ourselves in that manner or not. Even after we invite God to change us, the transformation is not immediate, and depending upon our residual resistance, the overt effects range from undetectable to miraculous.

Why Human Nature Matters

We love to be flattered. But if you want to think like Jesus, then you have to deal with reality. Step one is for you to realize that your first tendency is likely to be to deny letting God have His way with you, in you, and through you. The more completely you own the notion that your ways are not God's ways, the more hope there is that you will be able to abandon your free, selfish will in favor of His loving, perfect will.[39] This is a choice you must make. It does not happen without your involvement in the process.

Knowing the truth about your nature allows you to anticipate likely failings and to prepare accordingly. Do you scrutinize yourself throughout the day—your words, your attitude, your motivations, your behavior, your desires—to identify eruptions of inappropriateness? If your tendency is to be stubborn, rebellious, selfish, unfaithful, hypocritical and even wicked, do you care enough about your relationship with God to remain alert to such manifestations of ungodliness? How diligent are you in examining all facets of your life to locate instances of hypocrisy, arrogance, or sin? In anticipation of such eruptions, have you prepared solutions, such as a healthy prayer life, accountability partners, and sufficient knowledge of Scripture, to combat those evil impulses?

While working through this aspect of worldview development, I was struck again by the significance of knowing God's Word. Jesus did everything He could to ensure that we learned this lesson. When He was called upon to defend Himself, notice how often He referred to scriptural passages as His foundation. When He criticized religious leaders for bad counsel and modeling, it was on the basis of biblical principles that those leaders had ignored or distorted. How devoted are you to reading, studying, understanding, memorizing, and applying the Bible? If you want to think like Jesus, how closely does your personal decision-making and behavioral model reflect His as demonstrated in Scripture?

THE PLACE OF THE CHRISTIAN CHURCH

The entire population of followers of Jesus Christ, commonly known as the Church, plays a significant role in your understanding of the purpose of your life. Recall that in order to love God, we must love what He loves. His most cherished relationship is with people, so we, too, must be in relationship with each other, united through our common devotion to God.

The Church is the family of believers who share a common heritage in Adam and Eve and the nation of Israel, a common purpose in loving and obeying God, a common focus in the Bible, and a common hope in Jesus Christ. The most succinct description of the Church is provided in Acts 2, where we see the believers practicing their faith as Jesus commanded. The components of the early church were simple enough:

teaching, fellowship, prayer, communion, evangelism and outreach, baptism, miraculous signs and wonders, sharing of possessions, serving the needy, and worship. The attitude of the believers is described as reverent, joyous, and generous.[40]

Has the role of the Church changed in the past two thousand years? Not at all. The gathering of believers retains its traditional significance as a group of people—not a meeting place—who are united by their common bond in Jesus Christ, brought together to "equip God's people to do his work and build up the church, the body of Christ, until we come to such unity in our faith and knowledge of God's Son that we will be mature and full grown in the Lord, measuring up to the full stature of Christ."[41] Thus, our job is to come together to be better prepared to love God and people. That happens as we worship God together; share our faith in Him with nonbelievers; learn God's ways and embrace the qualities that enable us to embody those ways; wisely manage His resources for kingdom purposes; aggressively address the challenges facing needy people; and develop deep relationships with other believers that provide encouragement, accountability, and stability.

Why the Christian Church Matters

As you explore how to respond appropriately to the existence of God and how to make sense of your life, consider the role of the Church in your efforts. It has become fashionable for American Christians to downplay the need to be intimately involved in Church life, but the Bible is littered with references to our responsibility to actively participate in the Church. Particular aspects of our attempts to know, love, and serve God with all of our heart, mind, strength, and soul can be accomplished only through intentional and significant involvement in Church life.

In that regard, you cannot realize your complete purpose and meaning in life until you venture into a solid commitment to, and investment in, a body of believers. It is through such a connection that you are best able to know, love, serve, and obey God. And it is often through such a relationship with fellow followers of God that you become more tuned in to what you can expect to experience once your days on this planet are finished. The Bible tells us plenty about what will take place after we die on earth—and those critical insights into the coming phase of our existence will be considered in the next chapter.

Eight

QUESTION 5:

WHAT HAPPENS AFTER

WE DIE ON EARTH?

THE STORY IS TOLD of an encounter with the devil. Satan entered the home of a man, sat down on his couch, leaned forward with a big smile, and made his pitch.

"I'd like you to sell me your soul."

The man's eyes narrowed as he sized up the devil. "What are you prepared to offer?"

Still smiling, the evil one replied, "In exchange for your soul, I'll give you all the money you could ever want plus fame, power, and respect."

The man sat back in his chair and pondered the offer for several minutes. Finally he muttered out loud, "Hmmm, there must be a catch."

That man, along with millions of Americans, truly has no clue. The exchange summarizes the relative unimportance many people attach to their spiritual essence. Millions do not understand the existence and workings of evil, grace, salvation, the soul, Heaven, and Hell. Displaying typical American optimism, we assume that if we mean well and try hard, everything will work out for the best. That helps to explain why our national surveys consistently identify a paradox. On the one hand, most people have not confessed their sins and accepted Jesus Christ as their personal Savior. On the other hand, more than nine out of ten adults believe that when they die they will experience eternal life.[1] Of course, this is a contradiction only if you possess a biblical worldview. Otherwise, that pair of perspectives seem to fit together as naturally as eggs and bacon.

In a biblical worldview, then, what is the relationship of sin, forgiveness, grace, salvation, and one's soul?

TWO DIMENSIONS: PHYSICAL AND SPIRITUAL

Every person has two distinct but intimately related dimensions: the physical and the spiritual. Our physical existence is understood through our body; the Bible alludes to it as the heart and soul.[2] Our spiritual essence is manifest through our soul, which seems to be a non-material aspect of our being.[3] Scripture also asserts that your soul is the most important aspect of your existence because it is eternal and its vitality is directly related to your experience with God.[4]

Nurturing Your Soul

Your soul is invisible, but it is both sensitive and conscious. Just as your daily choices affect your physical condition, so do those choices affect your spiritual well-being.[5] You are not likely to feel completely fulfilled in life until your spiritual dimension is in balance—that is, until you have come to grips with your spiritual nature and achieved a sense of peace with God. In fact, we discover from Scripture that such fulfillment comes from adhering to God's commands and from investing in your relationship with God.[6] For instance, the Bible refers to the soul as thirsting for God, benefiting from wisdom, and experiencing intense emotions.[7] Not surprisingly, it undergoes emotions from joy to anguish in regard to its relationship with God.[8] Because we were created for a meaningful bond with God, when that relationship is not nurtured we innately suffer and feel uncomfortable. Spiritually speaking, your soul realizes emptiness and disappointment due to the unmet need that exists in your primary domain—the spiritual.[9]

Our society commonly jokes about the soul and treats it either as if it does not exist or it does not matter. Yet your soul reflects the deepest expression of your spiritual reality and experience.[10] There is an invisible yet seamless relation between heart, mind, and soul: You engage in thinking, speaking, and behaving through your physical being, but the final effect is experienced by your soul. Therefore, how you express interest in and commitment to loving and obeying God will determine your soul's ultimate outcome.[11]

After you die, your soul will continue to exist in an eternal state. What can you do to prepare your soul for a positive eternal experience?

THE PROBLEM OF EVIL AND SIN

As we've discussed in earlier chapters, God is pure and true. God is love. By His very nature He cannot put up with that which is evil and impure.[12] However, because He desires a genuine, unforced love-based relationship with the intelligent beings He has created, He allows those creatures—angels and people—to choose between seeking to honor and love Him or grasping for self-fulfillment and personal glory.

Satan's Rebellion

God's nature is so glorious that a group of His own angels, led by a rene-gade (the spiritual adversary we know as Satan), rebelled against God, seeking to overthrow His sovereignty. Satan's goal was—and is—to rule the universe, believing himself to be better suited for the job than its Creator. Backed by one-third of Heaven's angels, Satan battled God and His loyal angels—and lost. God cast Satan and all the rebel angels out of His presence. Nevertheless, God continues to rule over them even in their banishment. God uses Satan to test and refine humanity's love for Him.[13]

Satan is therefore devoted to two ends: undermining God and destroying God's creatures, humankind.[14] The evil one started his campaign with the first couple (Adam and Eve) and has continued to haunt humanity ever since. Scripture states that the legacy of Adam and

Eve is that we are born with a nature predisposed to sin and that the devil will continually tempt people to reject God and His ways until the end of time.[15] The devil and his followers will then be remanded to a "lake of fire" where they will be tormented for the duration of eternity.[16]

Until that time, though, we will be the primary objects of Satan's unwavering attention and evil designs. As a created being who must have God's permission to tempt people, Satan cannot cause us to sin; that is a choice we freely make.[17] The time-worn excuse—"the devil made me do it"—is theologically incorrect; the devil may persuade you to reject God's ways, but he cannot force you or make you do anything other than what you choose to do. God allows such temptations to occur in order to test our love and refine our faith. He never allows believers to be tempted beyond their capacity to resist.[18] He even provides us with various weapons with which to ward off the temptations, but even then the use of those resources is a personal choice that reveals the contours of our love for God.

What Is Sin?

Sin is rebellion against God's wishes and ways. It is our decision to disobey God's principles. While Satan gets credit for bringing us to the point of decision, the choice of doing evil is ultimately ours. We cannot blame circumstances, other people, or the spiritual world for our choices; we must own them.

The Bible clearly states that no human being has ever been able to resist sin for the duration of his or her life; every person sins against God.[19] These acts of treason against God are advanced by the craftiness of the devil. In his passion to destroy God's kingdom, Satan assails us with every weapon he has—and at every available opportunity. The Bible describes Satan's multiple strategies as including the distortion of Scripture and its interpretation, deception, implanting doubt, attracting us to the occult and to false gods, tempting us to pursue illegitimate forms of satisfaction, and by wearing us down with diligent attacks.[20]

Regardless of the motivation leading to sin, disobedience drives a wedge between our holy and loving God and us, fracturing the relationship He seeks to have with us and that we desperately need in order to experience the fullness and joy of life.[21] Too often we minimize the impact of sin, believing that any given sinful act is just another insignificant and forgettable event in a life filled with thousands and thousands of choices. But our determination to trivialize sin does not mean sin is unimportant. God takes *every* sin seriously because it indicates the sincerity of our commitment to Him.[22] Sin literally destroys our relationship with God; each sin is an offense against Him, even if it is unintentional.[23] Given His nature, no sin can go unpunished, although every sin that is confessed will be forgiven.[24] But without some type of radical mechanism of reconciliation, it is impossible for us to gain God's unmitigated favor and receive His eternal favor and blessings.

Sin Demands Judgment

Have you ever heard people portray their actions in ways designed to suggest that their sins were not significant because they had not committed "major" sins—murder, rape, armed robbery, or the like? The feeble euphemisms we sometimes cling to in order to excuse our faults— such as *white lies, a momentary lapse of judgment, a brief fling, sowing wild oats,* and *a moral stumble*—may make us feel better, but they still represent failures to live up to God's standards. Because every action has a related consequence, we must recognize that every sin must receive a response from the One who judges sin. His infinitely just nature mandates that the response be one of punishment through removal of His presence and blessing—unless we can somehow find a way to convince Him that our sins deserve to be overlooked.

Perhaps you've encountered people who feel as if their eternal outcome is rosy and secure because they are "good." In fact, my company's nationwide research consistently shows that Americans are more likely to believe

that God will be compelled to award them eternal favor if they are generally good people or have done enough good works during their lifetime
than they are to believe that their sins overshadow their deeds, shatter their
bond with God, and require some type of spiritual reconciliation with
Him. Foreseeing this possibility, God addressed this in the Bible. He states
in no uncertain terms that even our best efforts are insufficient to wipe out
the sinful desires of our hearts.[25] Instead, God insists that there be atone-
ment or reparation for our choice to rebel against Him.[26]

FORGIVENESS, GRACE, AND SALVATION

Recognizing how impossible it is for us to remain free from sin, but
unable to ignore sin, God determined that the only way for Him to enjoy
an unbroken relationship with us would be through the provision of a
permanent and encompassing sacrifice for our sins.[27] That, of course, is
what Jesus Christ's death on the cross represents for all who acknowledge and confess their sins, ask God for His forgiveness, and accept
Jesus' death and resurrection as a sacrifice on their own behalf.[28]

God's Grace through Jesus Christ

This incredible act of love by God—sending His perfect Son to earth to
take full responsibility for our sins and pay the price for our past, present,
and future bad choices—is the ultimate example of God's grace. Grace is
God's gift of love, initiated by God, to those who do not deserve such
favor.[29] It is that grace alone that enables us to have the assurance that
our soul will live forever with God, receiving His forgiveness, acceptance, blessings, and full adoption into His family. Without the vicarious
death of Jesus on our behalf we would not have any hope of eternal
reconciliation with God because we are too immersed in sin.[30]

When Jesus died on the cross, He did more than just expire with our
sins in tow; He conquered both death and the necessity of eternal

condemnation of all people through His resurrection and ascension back to His rightful place in Heaven with God.[31] His return to Heaven provides us with an advocate before the eternal Judge as well as the means to become a new form of humanity through the empowerment of the Holy Spirit, who lives within us once we confess our sins and turn our life over to Jesus.

Some people I have encountered over the years who are not Christians have expressed the feeling that sending one's son to die for other people's mistakes does not sound like the work of a trustworthy, loving God. They don't understand how Jesus' death was necessary to show the severe consequences of sin, to prove the consistency of His principles and responses, to underscore how incapable we are of determining our own destiny, and to provide an unequaled example of love and care. They simply do not have a clue how much sin matters to God, how much we matter to God, and how incredible was the sacrifice that He made on our behalf through Christ's death on that cross in Israel.

WHAT HAPPENS TO YOUR LIFE

Many Christians fail to realize that once they embrace Jesus as their Lord and Savior, their salvation experience has begun, even while they are still on earth. When we discuss salvation we tend to focus on the life we will experience after our physical death, but God produces immediate changes in our existence the moment we register our commitment to love and honor Him more fully by relying upon Jesus as our Savior.

Restored and Sanctified

Accepting God's grace is not merely "eternal fire insurance"—a kind of supernatural death benefit that kicks in after our funeral. Salvation introduces radical changes into our earthly experience as well. The Holy Spirit of God is sent to take up residence within us, providing power, guidance, and security that would otherwise be unavailable.[32] We can relax, knowing that we have received not only the forgiveness from our rebelliousness and the elimination of the eternal punishment due such misbehavior, but we are elevated to the status of "nuclear family" through God's spiritual adoption.[33] Theologians would posit that we are in the process of being "sanctified," implying that God is transitioning us to greater holiness through a progressive process of restoration.[34]

The evidence of this change of heart is seen in the "fruit" of repentance. People who genuinely turn their lives over to God, inviting and allowing Him to transform them through the presence and power of His Holy Spirit, are more likely to display evidence of that new way of living through their thinking and activity, and are less likely to engage in conversations and behaviors that dishonor God.[35] In fact, it is this tangible evidence of a renewed character and conduct that substantiates our claim that we have truly abandoned our life to Jesus.

Our spiritual rehabilitation does not mean we will neither sin nor be tempted to sin after embracing salvation. The devil is indiscriminate in his attacks against people, deriving pleasure from the misdirection of people whether or not they love Jesus. But God always provides us with the strength to resist Satan's invitations to sin and provides specific means of rejecting his overtures. Specifically, we are encouraged to pray for deliverance, to physically remove ourselves from the situation, or to boldly say no to the temptation. Just as God strengthened and ministered to Jesus after His times of temptation, so does He promise to enable us to do His will if we are determined to pursue it.[36]

POSTHUMOUS DESTINATIONS

After death we undergo the final judgment by God based upon the choice we made regarding the role of Jesus Christ in our life. Either we choose to rely upon Him as our means to eternal peace with God, or we choose to be independent and suffer God's everlasting condemnation for our unresolved sinfulness.

Hell

Those who try to make the most out of life without a life-saving connection to Jesus wind up going to Hell. Bible scholars are divided on exactly what "Hell" refers to. Some contend that Hell is a *place* of pain and suffering created by God for Satan and his followers, while others argue that it is not a physical location but a *state* of permanent separation from God's presence.[37] Either way, Scripture is clear that being in Hell is reserved for those who have chosen to either ignore God's rules or who thought they could impress Him with their goodness. Their error in judgment will cause them to endure everlasting punishment, suffering, and personal destruction.[38]

Hell is created for and experienced by three types of beings: Satan, his demons (who are the fallen angels defeated by God's angels), and people who reject Jesus' offer of grace.[39] It seems that everyone who is assigned to Hell will know pain and devastation through a combination of physical agony along with the emotional and spiritual torment that will result from alienation from God and His blessings. No matter what description of Hell you choose to adopt, it is an outcome that no one would want to experience for even the briefest of moments.[40]

Heaven

The more appealing alternative—and there are only two options in God's eternal multiple-choice test—is to spend eternity in Heaven. The Bible contains much more information about Heaven than it does about Hell, but there is still debate as to the exact nature of Heaven. It is clear that Heaven was created by God, is the home of all three persons of God (the Father, the Son, and the Holy Spirit) and His angels, and is ruled by

Him.[41] It is reserved for those who love, worship, serve, and obey God—including humans who believe in Jesus as their Savior.[42] It is a holy place and is a reward for those who are faithful to God, through their relationship with His risen Son.[43] Those who reside in Heaven will experience all the benefits of God's presence: peace, joy, love, fulfillment, and purity.[44]

Contrary to some teachings, it appears that those who go to Heaven receive a new body to accompany their soul. That body will be tailor-made for an eternity in God's presence, reflecting unique character traits, personality, and superior physical qualities. That heavenly body will never experience sickness or pain.[45] We will be citizens of this new and final home, enjoying God in all His glory and splendor—and putting our earthly travails and tribulations in perspective![46]

One of the Bible's more important points is that our final destination is more important than what we achieve during our time on earth, and spending the remainder of eternity in Heaven ought to be our present goal. Achieving the right to become a citizen of Heaven should be our primary aim in life.[47] The fact that such status cannot be bought, earned, or otherwise derived is incredibly clear; only through acceptance of Christ's atoning death on our behalf do we receive the privilege of being in Heaven for the rest of time.

WHY DOES ANY
OF THIS MATTER?

Your understanding of sin, surrender, salvation, and the soul have a dramatic influence on how you live. For instance, your response to sin—your belief in its existence, how seriously you take it, your desire to avoid it, your reaction to the commission of sins, your view of the temporal and spiritual affects of sin—has a direct correlation with your behavior, your spiritual commitment, and your relationship with God.

A Battle for Souls

In fact, how you understand and respond to sinful urges and behaviors is the deciding factor in the raging spiritual battle that is being waged for your soul. Every choice we make matters to God and has a personal effect; we have the capacity to resist sin, and we have no excuses for choosing not to do so. Gaining insight into the battle for your soul and for your role in that battle impacts the degree of freedom, joy, victory, and fulfillment you experience from moment to moment.

A biblical worldview would enhance your alertness to the battle. In my observation, the more aware you become of the nature, magnitude, and implications of the unseen battle for your soul, the more wary you become of everything you encounter. There are no accidents in life, there is no *luck*, and nothing is truly random. Although we will not have perfect understanding of every event that takes place in our life, we can be assured that everything happens for a purpose, and every action or choice is an important move in a spiritual chess game. Once you understand the game, the players, and the stakes, you become much more intentional in your moves. This is a game "for keeps." Winning is not everything in this game; it's the only thing.

In fact, if you truly comprehend the contours of this battle, then you must certainly recognize the awesomeness of God's love. Who else would have sent His own son to die a painful and unjust death on behalf of people who did not deserve another chance, much less a free ride for eternity? Who else would be so totally in love with us, and so desirous of an intense relationship with us, that He would analyze all of our dysfunctions and develop a relatively painless means out of our own frailties? Who else would see good in us that we cannot even see in ourselves—and fight to the finish to defend us from an adversary who would mercilessly exploit our weaknesses? Who else would make such abundant love and care available to everyone—and be willing to wait for those who are not interested in the hope that they might have a change of heart and embrace the One who embraced them first?

Motivation for Sharing God's Love

Indeed, if you understand these matters then you must also realize how horrible it would be to live without God at the center of your life. It would not be enough to know about Him, or to be interested in Him, or even to fear Him; Scripture reminds us that even the demons meet those requirements.[48] No, if you rightly perceive these things, then you are filled with a burning desire to respond to God in three significant ways: to love Him through worship, to love Him through obedience, and to love Him by encouraging others to fall to their knees before Him.

I suspect that we have relatively few believers in America who are zealous about the Great Commission precisely because so few of us truly comprehend the meaning of life without God. Most of us believers stumbled into His grace and are generally grateful for the gift of eternal life, but we have not fully absorbed the dimensions of His love for us. Those who do grasp the full scope of His love are overwhelmed and radically transformed. Not only does their worldview change, but also everything in their life is permanently altered by the outrageous magnitude of His love for us.

If you secretly wonder whether or not you "get it"—and it's perfectly reasonable and healthy to wonder such a thing, even if you do understand—I suppose the best way to discover the answer is to figure out what you are living for. As you think about what you did today, how often were you focused on doing things that you consciously believed would honor and please God versus how many things you pursued in order to satisfy your own needs and desires, or those of the people around you? How often did you intentionally respond to a situation in ways that reflect your perception of Heaven's eternal yardstick rather than out of the hope of achieving immediate gratification? How often was your effort related to maximizing current opportunities rather than storing up "treasures in Heaven"?

Living in a Land of Cheap Grace

We Americans live in the land of cheap grace; we gladly accept peace with God through Jesus' death and resurrection, but we assume no responsibility for change because we argue that we did not agree to that requirement beforehand and would find an alternative route to God's palace anyway. So deep-rooted is our denial of reality—even among those of us who are blessed enough to know Jesus as a personal Savior—that we fail to recognize that His terrible death on that splintered wooden cross was not our gateway to Spiritual Easy Street.

If we are determined to live for God's purposes and glory rather than our own we must experience personal brokenness over our history and inclination to sin. We must wholly abandon ourselves to God. In practical terms, that means giving up our agendas, our dreams, and our plans in order to listen for His quiet voice that leads us toward a very different and unworldly future. It may not be a future of voluntary poverty like Mother Teresa or devotion to preaching the gospel á la Billy Graham. But that small voice that whispers so urgently to you in the clutter of the daily cacophony will lead you to transform every thought, word, and action in ways that would not otherwise be possible or plausible. The outcome—greater godliness, more consistent holiness, ever-developing selflessness—is the result of someone who understands the ravages of sin, the burden of guilt, the freedom of God's grace, the joy of peace with God, and the reformation of a renewed heart and mind.

If it is true, as I have suggested, that you become what you believe, then the more you understand the power of sin, of forgiveness, of spiritual rebirth, and of the permanent peace and pleasure that await you in

Heaven, the more you will become one who acts like Jesus because you are able to think like Jesus. That capacity will help you to make sense out of moral truth, the topic we will tackle in our next chapter.

Nine

QUESTION 6:

WHAT SPIRITUAL AUTHORITIES EXIST?

EVERY DAY IS DIFFERENT, but most of my days have a streak of common elements that course throughout them. After waking up grudgingly at the last possible moment, I mechanically dispense with the morning necessities—hygiene, dressing, breakfast—and begin to think about how to be the most productive during the day. At the office I narrow my sights onto the plans and communications that will determine the apparent success or failure of my efforts. After work hours, my focus is devoted to enjoying my family, accomplishing necessary household tasks, and completing any unfinished business before checking e-mail, sports scores, and then collapsing into bed.

In other words, on most days I am shockingly oblivious to what is really happening in me, around me, and through me.

Sure, I pray at various times throughout the day. I typically pause before making key decisions to listen for God's quiet but unmistakable voice. I even throw some God-talk into my conversations with employees, clients, and family members. But for the most part, I am totally distracted and even naïve about the spiritual battle that rages in my midst. Most of the believers I know fare no better at being sensitive to the severe spiritual combat in progress.

Invisible Battles

Contrary to my perceptions, the true purpose of my day is not related to making money, loving my family, caring for my body, achieving happiness, or growing intellectually. My life—and yours—is all about engagement in the eternal struggle between good and evil, the no-holds-barred confrontation between holiness and sin.[1] Every event in my day is merely the context within which the next battle in that war occurs.

Astonishingly, my role in the war matters to my Deity in Chief although my personal contribution to the war will not change the final outcome one iota. It is only because of my commander's inexhaustible love for me that my choices in the war have any meaning whatsoever.

So when I interact with a colleague at work, there are invisible forces competing for my attention and loyalty throughout the conversation, striving to influence me to further their competing agendas. While I write an analysis of survey data, there is a tug of war for control of my mind as a battle rages between the forces that promote truth and those that promote deception and distortion. Each time I enter a store and evaluate the merchandise, there is an unseen tussle in me between those who want me to waste God's resources and those who fight for their responsible use. When I stretch out on the couch at night to see if there is anything worthwhile on the television, my channel surfing is not as random as I might like to think: There are powers battling each other to get me to choose particular types of programming because of the effect the content will have upon my life and character.

And there is no escape from these immortal enemies as they drag me into the conflict; they will find me no matter where I go, no matter what my last response was, no matter how old I grow, no matter what my spiritual leanings of the moment might be. These armies play for keeps, and even though my battle record is incidental to the ultimate (already-determined) outcome, each side makes a play for my allegiance as if its success depended upon winning me over. Every moment of every day we are at war.[2]

THE ULTIMATE STEALTH WAR

Those who possess competing worldviews would like you to believe that this is just a fantasy conflict conjured up by people with creative imaginations or adhered to by weaklings who fear their own shadow. Seductive as such naysaying may be, it is a recipe for personal destruction because we are warriors in the most inclusive, longest-running, continuous battle of all time: the battle for people's spiritual affections.

This is the ultimate stealth war. The combatants are invisible, the weapons are powerful, and there is an inexhaustible supply of ammunition. It pits the two most powerful forces in existence in a fight to the finish: the army of God versus the legions of Satan. Oddly, you and I are the final contestants drawn to the battlefield. The prize to the victor: dominion over human souls and unfettered authority over all creation.[3]

One of the strangest elements of this war, however, is that we will fight until the end yet with full knowledge of the outcome. There is no dispute about the end result: God wins! We know that there will be casualties along the way, but God and His ways will emerge victorious, and His purposes will be accomplished. Millions of people—perhaps even you and I—will be bloodied or even lost in the war, but God will remain the undefeated, undisputed champion of the universe.

We have been given the freedom to choose our side: God's victory-bound army or Satan's Hell-bound band of live-for-the-moment losers. It doesn't take much brainpower to realize that siding with God is the only intelligent choice in this exercise. And yet God's adversary is skilled; Satan deceives and seduces literally hundreds of millions of people throughout the world, convincing them to reject God's offer of eternal love and redemption in favor of Satan's offer of pleasure in this world. We sign on with God's army by embracing Jesus Christ as our Lord and Savior and following His guidance to live in accordance with His will. As in every war, it's not as easy a task as it sounds—the enemy is wily, diligent and more capable than we are—but if we make a good choice and persevere in our efforts to follow the commands given by our Leader, we will enjoy the spoils of victory with God in Heaven. We serve a Leader who never forgets those who have been fully loyal—and One whose nature makes it impossible for Him to forgive those who have rejected His offer of salvation.[4]

In this spiritual warfare we can rely upon perspectives and promises provided to us by our Deity in Chief. He tells us that even though we have become key players in the battle action, this is not about us; it's about the will of the leaders of the opposing forces. When we choose to be on God's side, we do not wage our own battle. We are soldiers in His army fighting His battle.[5] Consequently, we must fight God's battle with His plans and weapons, relying upon Him for direction and provision.[6]

Victory Despite Setbacks

He assures us that we will emerge victorious if we trust fully in Christ, demonstrate our complete faith in and allegiance to Him by living a holy life, and use the resources He provides to fend off the attacks of the enemy. This is a war we cannot win on our own power; it requires the strength of God's Holy Spirit residing within and working through us to overcome the destructive efforts of God's eternal foe.[7]

No matter how committed we are to fighting the good fight of faith, we will suffer minor setbacks along the way.[8] This is to be expected, but it ought not derail us from our plan; we must stay focused on God's will, fight for we believe to be significant and true, and retain assurance that God will prevail. Victory comes to each of us through our commitment to God demonstrated through our daily engagement in the struggle against evil and our determination to finish well and to remain faithful and obedient regardless of the cost.[9]

Truth be told, you and I are in way over our heads. We do not have the intelligence, the resources, or the natural ability to win the war, so we must choose a side and fight for that cause.[10] Because we have been given a sensitive conscience as part of our makeup, we innately know which side is just and appropriate—but we have the freedom to choose either side, for whatever reasons. Either way, we will receive reinforcements. If you declare yourself for the forces of evil, Satan becomes your master and his demons will direct your paths. If you choose God's side, you will be guided by His Holy Spirit and assisted by His angels. And we have ultimate authority over the enemy through our connection with Jesus Christ.[11] Exercising that authority may not be easy, but the authority is real and accessible and can be wielded effectively.

A ROSTER OF COMBAT PERSONNEL

Take a closer look at these unseen powers and authorities in the invisible battle for your soul and the continuing fight for eternal supremacy.

The Holy Spirit

The Holy Spirit is to the Trinity what Zeppo Marx was to the Marx Brothers: the forgotten member of the trio. Mention Holy Spirit, and people nod in knowing affirmation; ask them to describe the nature and being of God, and the "third person" is suddenly the mystery man, the odd man out.

Make no mistake about it, though: The Holy Spirit is God.[12] It is through this form that God is present with us, fulfills His new covenant with us, and continues to influence the world to draw closer to Him.[13] Scripture confirms that the Holy Spirit possesses all the character qualities we identify as being of God—omnipresence, omniscience, holiness, and so forth.[14] If you understand the nature and purposes of God, then you understand the nature and purposes of the Holy Spirit. It is the

Spirit that facilitates our experiencing of God's will, guidance, qualities, and kingdom in diversified ways.

If we perceive God to be the creative founder of the universe who is "in charge," and Jesus Christ to be the Son sent to rescue us from ourselves, it is the Holy Spirit who gives us the power and capacity to live up to our spiritual promise. How does He do that? By living within us and expressing Himself through our conscience, dreams, visions, miracles, healings, even direct speech—any means that will capture our attention and convey His holy desire for us.[15]

God wants every person on earth to have His Spirit in his or her heart, but He can only take up residence in those who have confessed their sinfulness and inadequacy and asked for the forgiveness, acceptance, and empowerment available through Jesus.[16] One of the Spirit's primary functions, then, is revealing God's standards, bringing our sins to our attention, and calling us to change our ways and seek His forgiveness.[17] The Spirit is then awarded as God's gift to those loved ones as the confirmation of His approval, protection, and provision.[18]

The gifts provided by the Holy Spirit are plentiful. The Bible liberally identifies those blessings as new life, power, joy, truth, inspiration, protection, comfort, love, direction, peace, goodness, wisdom, help, strength, and supernatural abilities.[19] Take the time to consider each of these remarkable presents delivered to us through the Spirit's activity and marvel at how magnificently God has addressed all of our needs and best interests.

The Spirit also reveals God's plans to us so that we may be obedient and sufficiently equipped to serve Him.[20] The Spirit prays for us both as an intercessor and in confirmation of our requests and praises, conversing with God the Father in ways we cannot understand or imitate.[21]

Amazingly, many people resist the Holy Spirit.[22] Some do so through persistent sin, some through denial of the Spirit's existence, others via dogged disinterest in God and His purposes. The Spirit never forces Himself upon anyone, but neither will He suffer the insults of fools.

Indeed, the only "unforgivable sin" mentioned in Scripture is that of grieving the Holy Spirit—often interpreted to mean the flat-out dismissal, repudiation, or insulting of Jesus Christ.[23] After what Jesus endured for each person, to denigrate His unsurpassable act of love is deemed the final straw that casts such individuals as the eternal enemy of God, sealed through abandonment by the Holy Spirit.

To win the spiritual battle, you must have God on your side. Through the presence of His Holy Spirit living within you, ushered into your heart upon your admission and confession of sin, and your determination to love God with all your heart, mind, strength, and soul, you have the power to be transformed and to be a transforming presence for God's glory throughout the world.

Angels

Americans love angels, or the humanized caricatures they think are angels. The angels spoken of in the Bible are vastly different. Although we have something in common with them—both angels and humans are created by God and exist to love, obey, and serve Him—the similarities end there.[24]

Angels preceded us in the creation saga and clearly surpass human ability in many areas.[25] However, because they were created expressly for the purpose of worshiping God, it seems that their praise is not entirely satisfying to God; He desires the awe and respect of beings who have a broader range of choices and freely decide to worship and glorify Him. Their worship does please Him, though, and they remain at His beck and call, doing His will in the heavenly realm or here on our planet.[26]

The Bible makes numerous references to the appearance and influence of angels. They are described as numerous, perfect and holy, mighty, and discerning.[27] They rejoice when sinners repent of their folly in favor of godly living, and they devote most of their existence to praising God.[28]

We do not normally consider angels to be confrontational or directive, but that is sometimes how God chooses to use them. There are many instances in which these supernatural beings confronted, guided, warned, or directly cared for specific individuals.[29] Sometimes their presence or impact on a life directly leads to a person's decision to follow Christ.[30]

Angels affect our lives in significant but undetectable ways. For instance, God sends them to convey messages, protect us, equip us for success and endurance, and to encourage and comfort us.[31] Angels provide us with insight, wisdom, and discernment necessary to make appropriate decisions.[32] In the process they sometimes reveal the future to us; whether we have the wisdom and courage to capitalize on such revelation is another matter altogether![33] These spirits have been known to provide physical help and strength when needed.[34] And children, who clearly have a special place in God's heart, even have special angels—the proverbial "guardian angels"—to ensure their safety and development.[35]

But an angel's work with humans is not all fun and peaceful. The Bible notes that angels are used by God to divert evil activity, destroy those who would hinder God's plan or block His purposes, and to punish those who persist in doing evil.[36] During the end times, God will use angels to separate the good from the evil so that each might have an appropriate conclusion.

Although it may seem as if angels do not get the credit they deserve for their invaluable intervention, it seems that they generally do not act of their own accord; more often than not, it appears they are sent by the Lord to do His bidding.[37] The end result for believers, however, is consistent: We are always better off because of their intervention in our lives.

Satan

If the created universe consisted only of God the Father, Jesus the Son, the Holy Spirit, and God's angels, what a joyous and carefree experience we would have. Unfortunately, the counterpart to God's purity and holiness thrives in this created world through the leadership of a fallen angel we know as Satan. For thousands of years the evil one has been the thorn in the flesh of humanity, although when God is ready, Satan's presence will be eliminated from the experience of believers.[38]

Satan was one of the angels created by God to praise Him for eternity. However, it appears that angels have enough freedom and character to go bad. As we discussed in chapter 8, Satan led a rebellion against God. The prideful angel thought he was more deserving of angelic praise than God and would be able to outmaneuver the Creator. Obviously, Satan overestimated himself and underestimated God, resulting in banishment from Heaven (giving special meaning to the phrase "pride comes before a fall").[39]

God has granted Satan the right to rule the earth for a period of time.[40] The evil one uses the opportunity to attack people, especially Christians, in the hope of stealing them from God's hand and attracting a sufficient following to eventually topple God's kingdom.[41] If Satan had any real hope of upending God, though, that hope was forever dashed by the resurrection of Jesus Christ, which proved God's mastery over sin and death.[42]

God retains control and authority over Satan at all times, simply allowing the banished angel to test and perfect the faith of people. Satan has limited capabilities and cannot do anything without God's permission; after all, he is not a deity.[43] For instance, even though Satan is much smarter than we are, he is not omniscient and is therefore unable to foresee the future or read our minds. As a spiritual being, he covers lots of ground quickly, but unlike God, he is not omnipresent.[44] His effect on our lives is largely the result of taking bold, strategic action, relying upon stunning craftiness, an incredible talent for deceiving and disarming people, and a deep-rooted hatred for truth.[45] His impact is magnified by his extreme nature: He is completely evil, totally hostile to anything created by God, and absolutely merciless in his attacks on people.[46] Although the death and resurrection of Jesus Christ was clearly a stunning, if not terminal, blow to his plans, Satan remains focused on his goal of outsmarting God and over-throwing Him once and for all. He views human beings as vehicles to be used in bringing God to His knees.

Satan's strategies for undermining people are well known yet so brilliantly executed that they remain effective thousands of years after their initial unveiling. He is able to create doubt about God and His commands; he is superb at distorting Scripture; he is a world-class deceiver; and he tempts us with fascinating exploits of darkness, such as the occult and sorcery.[47] One of the secrets to his success in causing us to stumble is his perseverance; he just does not give up![48] Perhaps that is because he realizes he is fighting a losing battle but wants to take as many of God's loved ones down with him as he can.

Some unfortunate individuals fall prey to satanic possession. Until the 1973 movie *The Exorcist* made it a national spectacle, possession—being under the complete influence of the devil—was not widely known or discussed by the public. But it is both real and biblically authenticated. When Satan chooses to possess someone, he may cause unbelievable pain, suffering, and loss of control.[49]

Usually, however, Satan's means are much less dramatic than possession. Seduction is one of his favorite ploys. The biblical record, certainly confirmed by human history, suggests that sexual temptations are his chief means of destroying people's lives. But he is capable of, and willing to use, any temptation that will lead to sin and personal degradation.[50] His method is to probe until he finds a weakness then to use that soft spot to gain a foothold in the person's life. From there he expands his evil influence.[51]

An accomplished actor, he imitates God whenever feasible—portraying himself as an "angel of light" to trick people into doing what is clearly against God's will but has been brilliantly portrayed as being consistent with God's desires.[52] The various names by which he is known in Scripture say it all: Accuser, Prince of Demons, Evil One, Father of Lies, Deceiver.[53]

Americans minimize the evil nature of Satan because we tend to be a relatively passionless culture—the result of Satan's lulling us to comfort and complacency about virtually everything in life. Most Americans do not understand the intensity of the devil's evil nature. In moral and spiritual terms, the Bible is unequivocal: Satan is the polar opposite of our loving, forgiving, holy God. Envision the most venomous, hateful, wicked person your imagination can conceive of—and realize that you have just scratched the surface on how intense, vile, and malignant Satan is.

As you wrap your mind around the nature of the spiritual battle and the central combatants, remember that this battle is not about you. You are caught in the crossfire of good and evil. Satan does not care about you at all; you are just a means to his impossible ends. Only God cares enough about you to ensure that you have the avenues and authority available to escape the clutches of this despicable creature.

Satan's Demons

Because he is limited in power and ability, Satan relies upon demons—other fallen angels who joined him in rebelling against God—to help him accomplish his goals. Demons were doomed from the beginning. they were followers of a fatally flawed leader and outnumbered by God's angels by a two-to-one margin. Life has been torturous for them ever since their unceremonious exit from the heavenly realm.

Just as there are some angels that are stronger or more powerful than others, so it seems that demons are a formidable but less powerful version of their former peer and current leader (Satan). They also are able to inhabit people, and when they do so they can inflict torture and pain.[54] They imitate their leader by conveying false teaching and by deceiving people with tricks and miracles.[55] But, like their leader, they are destined to defeat and to spending the remainder of time with him in Hell.[56]

Believers have been given the power to dominate demons if they appropriate the power of God and bind or cast out demons in the name of

Jesus Christ.[57] Like Satan, demons have no independent source of power or authority; they are able to do what God allows them to do, but they are always subject to His authority, commands, and name.[58] Jesus taught His followers that they have the power to banish demons if they do so in the proper manner. In fact, demonstrating God's power over demons is one of the paths that has led many people to Christ over the years.[59]

Demons cannot separate us from God's love or plan; only we can make the choice to disobey or depart from His will. But demons can be counted on to do everything in their power to persuade us to join them in their rebellion against God. Their success is wholly dependent upon our willingness to snub God and His ways.[60]

Just as we have tarnished the image of angels by turning them into cartoon characters, so have we minimized the threat of demons by caricaturing them. But make no mistake about it: Demons are powerful, wicked, clever, and resourceful spirits intent upon destroying you. That is their job, their reason for existence, and the only outcome that their leader accepts.

IMAGES OF THE WAR

Have you developed a mental image of the invisible war that defines and encompasses your life? In some ways the war is a joke; it pits the undefeated, indefatigable, mightiest ruler of all time (God) against an undermanned, overmatched egotist (Satan) backed by a ragtag group of nomad losers. The sides are so imbalanced that there is not a chance—not even a sliver of hope—that the underdog could pull off the unimaginable, a repeat of David versus Goliath. This war was over before it began. By definition, history, and any other measure you select, nobody beats God. Nobody.

But the history of war teaches an important lesson: When the vanquished foes feel they have nothing to lose, they either surrender immediately to salvage some vestige of their miserable existence, or they dig in for a bitter resolution to their plight, seeking to take down as many innocent people as they can before they meet their demise. You and I are those innocent bystanders who are caught in the sniper fire. Satan and his demons know they cannot defeat God, but they also know they can break His heart by snatching us away for a minute, a day, a year, or even for eternity by causing us to sin. As the apostle Paul wrote, our only hope is to utilize the protective gear that God provided for us: Scripture, prayer, commitment, truth, faith, and the power of the Holy Spirit.[61]

Choose Carefully: It Makes All the Difference

Grasping the nature of God and the other players in this eternal drama highlights the fact that this is not just a religious game or a Sunday sport: living the faith in the midst of this war is a twenty-four/seven challenge to us and a timeless tussle for the spirits involved. As one pastor described this during a sermon, "God's got a designer watch with no hands on it." Neither He nor the other celestial beings track time; to them, the final outcome is all that matters, and only God knows when time is up.

Comprehending this eternal battle is also incredibly humbling for us Americans, for we are *not* the centerpiece of the war! Granted, God loves us dearly and will do everything in His power to encourage us to fight according to His rules and for His purposes, but no matter how you look at it we are just bit players in an epic production. We need to know our place in the grand scheme and dutifully and thankfully play our minor role—"sinner seeking grace, holiness, and servanthood"—to the hilt.

An Eternal Perspective

Among other things, that may serve to reduce much of the tension and pressure we feel in relation to life. Our work is an assignment from God, and we honor Him by doing everything with excellence—but whether we make budget forecasts or get the top employee rating pales in comparison to how we fulfill our responsibility in the grand drama of good versus evil. The level of comfort we achieve may seem like a big deal as we drive through the neighborhood checking out other people's homes and cars, but one second after we die that information is forever lost and more important matters assume their rightful place of priority. Toning our bodies and building a network of helpful peers may be challenges, but we receive new bodies and a better network of contacts once our old bodies cease breathing. If our purpose is to love, obey, and serve, and if we recognize our place in the eternal battle for souls and allegiance, then many of our self-imposed crises fade into oblivion as fast as we can fabricate them.

Perspective is everything as we construct our worldview. In that process, do not fail to realize just how dreadful a nemesis Satan is. Not only is he real, but his character and objectives make Saddam Hussein, Osama bin Laden, Idi Amin, and Adolf Hitler look like grade-school bullies. He is the ultimate villain, the epitome of evil, the quintessential model of lawlessness. And he wants to get you. You should be scared— very scared—unless you have completely abandoned yourself to the Lord of creation. Even then, God warns you to be alert and ready to fend off Satan's inevitable advances.

AN APPRECIATION OF WHAT JESUS DID

Studying Satan's history, nature, and purposes has renewed my deep appreciation for what Jesus did by taking away my sins and eradicating the power of Satan over sinners who repent. What hope would there be otherwise? What would stop the evil one from having his wicked way with us forevermore? Coming to grips with the alternative has restored some of my lost gratitude for and commitment to Jesus for His sacrificial death for me. I shudder when I think about where I'd be without that escape mechanism. And I continue to shudder when I think about the lives of family and friends who habitually turn Him away, not cognizant of the abominable option they have thereby accepted by default.

Your adversary hates your guts and will do whatever he can to torment and shred you. Rest assured that at the very least he will search out your weaknesses and diligently exploit them.[62] How committed are you to identifying those shortcomings and relying on the grace and power of God to shore up those vulnerable areas? Most often, when we lose ground it is because of character flaws, but we must also examine the purity of our beliefs, the depth of our commitment, the submission of our will to God, our devotion to loving and serving others, and so forth. If there is a weak link in your chain—and there is; we all have them—then Satan will discover it and attack it. Be prepared to respond as God recommends: through the study and application of His word, through prayer, and through full reliance upon the power of His Holy Spirit to fend off the attack.

Every choice you make matters. You can enhance your choices by allowing the Holy Spirit, who is resident within you (if you are a genuine disciple of Jesus), to do the heavy lifting for you. You can rest assured that God will use His Spirit and His angels to protect you from attacks that transcend your ability to respond. And you can be supremely confident that until you take up residence in Heaven, Satan and his minions will attack you hour after hour, in ways big and small, overt and covert. Why? Because you are inextricably involved in the war to end all wars between the most powerful and ferocious of enemies. How well do you understand the stakes, the players, their positions, and your role and opportunities?

Ten

---◦◦◦---

QUESTION 7:

WHAT IS TRUTH?

EVERY WORLDVIEW HINGES ON an understanding of moral truth. To nihilists, there is no moral truth, and their attitudes and behaviors spring from that assumption. To postmodernists, all truth is relative to the individual and circumstances, resulting in self-absorbed attitudes and selfish behavior. To pantheists, each individual is a unique and complete embodiment of truth, leading to a life characterized by overconfidence and outlandish self-centeredness. But to the Christian, there are absolute moral truths that should not be violated because to do so attacks the character and purposes of God, who is the source and judge of all moral truth. To adopt God's truths leads to a life of significance; to reject His truths can only result in punishment.

Every worldview hinges on its concept of moral truth. Americans may not seem nearly as concerned about truth and personal morality as they are about physical comfort, emotional security, personal image, and material achievement. But every decision we make ultimately relates to our perceptions of truth. Because truth reflects what you believe to be indisputably accurate, your notion of truth is at the core of your understanding of and response to reality. In other words, for a worldview to help you make sense of reality and lay a foundation for your understanding of meaning, purpose, value, and righteousness, it must specify what truth is (or isn't).

THE APPLICATION OF TRUTH

In my philosophy courses in college and graduate school, truth was an abstract ideal we argued over without any sense that there might be an absolute standard to grasp and embrace. Our involvement was really more of a mental training exercise than a route to wisdom and discernment based on a true comprehension of the eternal importance of the matter. Whether we left a classroom debate siding with Socrates, Nietzsche, Sartre, Descartes, Locke, or Marx, we were pretty much convinced that there could not be moral absolutes given the nature of humanity and the realities of the world. Our conclusions were more often than not based on how persuasive someone's argument had been on a certain position or in response to how well a perspective paralleled one's personal inclinations. In my experience, colleges and universities these days are even more likely to lead students to conclude that absolute moral truth does not exist. I was just one among the millions of earnest students duped into such thinking over the past quarter century.

Little did I realize that such a position produces a domino effect. It was not until many years later—after accepting Christ and spending many hours reading and reflecting on the Bible—that I began to put the pieces together more intelligently. It finally dawned on me that if there is no such thing as absolute moral truth, then there can be no such thing as right or wrong. Without right and wrong, the idea of sin is baseless because it assumes a standard that is either upheld or broken. If sin does not exist, then you concurrently remove the notions of judgment and condemnation. Remove those elements from the discussion, and you also erase the need for a savior, for we have nothing to be saved from and no consequences to seek to avoid. Without the existence of sin and its ramifications, the death and resurrection of Jesus Christ are historically insignificant and personally meaningless.

As you might imagine, reaching that end brought me to a crossroads in my faith. Is Jesus truly the Savior of humanity? Does God really hold us accountable for our actions, and if so, on what basis? Does anything I do in this lifetime really matter? How can a person know what is true?

THE FOUNDATION OF TRUTH

As a believer in Christ and a servant of God, my worldview is based on the Bible. But in discussions with those who endorse alternative worldviews—or who simply want to critique a biblical worldview—the conversation often comes down to what each of us considers to be our core truths and the source of knowledge related to those elements. Inevitably—and appropriately—Christians must be able to defend the authority and reliability of the Bible as our source document for God's truth.

The Bible is unique in many ways. First, it claims to be God's direct revelation to us regarding His values, principles, and expectations.[1] Second, the words in the Bible come directly from God—written by people who were specifically directed by God in relation to the content.[2] While the personality, background, and context of each author is evident in what he wrote, the substance was from God. Third, because these are the words of a deity who is always truthful and accurate, the content represents truth for humankind.[3] Finally, Scripture is authoritative because it presents *God's* words to us—that is, they are the words of One who reigns over those whom He has created and whose commands are to be carried out precisely as He intends.[4]

Questions about the Bible

Conscientious objectors—some of whom are favorably disposed to Christianity—nevertheless raise some valid questions and concerns about the Bible. For instance, some critics note that a biblical principle can be abused by using it in ways not intended by God. This is a reasonable objection. God's words, while powerful and true, must be interpreted within their intended context. Indeed, if the Bible contains truth, there is no need to embellish the information; it will speak and stand up for itself, as God sees fit.

Another concern is that we do not have the original manuscripts of the Bible and therefore cannot trust the text we today call the Bible. This would indeed be problematic if it were not for the scrupulous manner in which the original manuscripts were copied and thus preserved by ancient scribes. The original texts were considered holy documents that had to be precisely maintained and handed down to subsequent generations. Accordingly, an entire class of "super scribes" emerged whose sole vocation in life was to perfectly preserve the content of the original documents.

Because the Bible was originally recorded on perishable materials, this painstaking hand-copying process went on for hundreds of years. To safeguard the accuracy of the materials, duplication was checked more thoroughly than most of us can imagine. Every letter, every syllable, every word, and every paragraph was counted, checked, and then re-checked multiple times by different quality-control specialists.

Further, because the Bible was deemed to be so special, numerous exact copies were made so that the content could be shared with people in as many places as possible. The result is an amazing number of remaining copies that serve to verify the consistency and accuracy of the copies made throughout the years. Scholars who have studied the preservation process emerge with little doubt that what survived throughout the centuries—until the advent of the printing press and the subsequent mass distribution of biblical content —provides little reason to question the accuracy of the content.

A concern that troubles many observers relates to the authority of the Bible. A document may proclaim itself to be true or to have been written by a specific author, but the mere claim of authenticity does not substantiate its authenticity. What reasonable evidence exists to support the striking claim that the Bible is the actual words of God?

Ever since the time the original manuscripts were written, various Jewish and Christian faith communities have upheld the claim that the Bible came directly from God. This unbroken, centuries-old chain of support for the Bible enhances its claim of authenticity. Others note that the individuals who were inspired by God to write the words that appeared on the page as God's own made no bones about the fact that the content was from God.

What made those claims most impressive, of course, was that the content written by God's chosen scribe was often written at great personal cost. (The writings of the prophets are a prime example: Recording harsh critiques and making dire threats of destruction to the rulers, armies, and culture in which they lived brought on beatings, imprisonment, banishment, and even death. Only those who were absolutely convinced that they were being called by God to communicate such messages would feel compelled to do so.) In addition, many authors of books in the Bible support the authenticity of the claims of fellow authors, citing them as responsible representatives of God's words.

One of the most impressive substantiations of the authority of the Bible, however, is that it possesses the attributes of that which scholars have agreed are the elements of truth. For instance, the Bible is internally consistent and unified in its principles and claims. There is also tremendous coherence across the many authors and centuries during which the various books were written and in which its stories unfold. Further, the fact that the information remains so compelling, dignified, and relevant to all the cultures of the world many centuries after it was written speaks to the timeless and universal wisdom of its Author.

Jesus Christ Endorsed the Bible

Personally, the most convincing argument is that Jesus Christ taught that the Bible is God's authoritative words to humankind. By personally endorsing the value and veracity of the Scriptures, Jesus empowers us to be totally confident that the Bible is reliable and authoritative.

How did Jesus endorse the Bible? In His teaching He frequently quoted passages of the Old Testament or based His lessons upon stories contained in those books. When He argued with religious leaders and teachers, His tendency was to draw them back to Scripture and rely upon the authority of the Word—and the result was that they resented being shown up but could neither contradict the wisdom nor challenge the source.[5] Most convincing is that He lived in strict accordance with the Law and its related principles, verifying the place of Scripture in His mind and heart.

We must concede that Jesus did not give direct consent to the truth of New Testament, since those books were not written until several decades after His resurrection. However, He had a direct hand in the development of those books by appointing the disciples who wrote them and giving them the knowledge, experience, and authority to speak in His name. Put it together: Each apostle was called by Jesus, had first-hand observation and experience related to His life and ministry, was filled with the Holy Spirit to facilitate God's wisdom and power to fulfill this incredible function, and was affirmed in his spiritual authority by the rest of the Church during that era.

A Bible for All Time

Some critics of the Bible argue that it seems improbable that a holy, omnipotent, and eternal God would resort to such an unreliable and simplistic means of communication as the written word. Why wouldn't He rely upon a more sophisticated means of getting His thoughts across to us?

Consider the big picture. We know that God existed before humankind and created a world that seemed incomplete. He filled the apparent void by creating people. He made people specifically to have a relationship with them. Because He wanted us to genuinely love Him, He could not create us in such a way that we were forced to love Him; our response to Him had to be our choice or else whatever love He received would be contrived and insignificant rather than meaningful and special. But by giving us the ability to make moral choices, He gave humans the chance to select sin rather than holiness. To enable us to deal with our poor choices, and to understand the context of our sin, He determined to provide a guidebook that would explain His original intent, what eventually happened, and what can be done to restore the possibilities in our lives.

Thus, God took the initiative to ensure that people of all races and regions would have access to His thoughts and principles. He did so because He wants to relate to us, but you cannot have a relationship without communication. In His omniscience, He recognized that having written documentation of His laws, commands, and principles would be far superior and more permanent than relying upon the preferred teaching method of the day (oral communication) or other means uniquely available to Him (dreams, visions, and so on).

I have heard someone state that if the Bible were truly God's message to us, He would have updated both the message and the delivery vehicles to reflect modern times and to seem more relevant. God has not done so, however, because His message has remained relevant throughout every age of history; His truth is timeless and universal. He could will into existence videotapes or CD-ROMs or DVDs of His message, but why do so? The written word has remained the heart of human communication for thousands of years and is still at the center of information dissemination today. He has not changed the message because it remains more accessible than ever in written form, its content is still perfect and life-changing, and His followers have translated those written words into every other form of communication known to humanity. Maybe that provides us with an unexpected lesson about influence: If what you've created works, don't mess with it![6]

THE BIBLE'S
COMMENTS ON TRUTH

Pontius Pilate, the Roman governor who facilitated the unlawful death of Jesus, listened to the religious leaders' charges against Jesus of

Nazareth but was unable to persuade them to handle the matter without his intervention. Grudgingly, he had the unkempt nomadic leader brought into his chambers. After a brief exchange, the shackled Savior explained His purpose. "I came to bring truth to the world. All who love the truth recognize that what I say is true." Showing his disinterest in the matter, Pilate responded sarcastically, "What is truth?" before turning Jesus over to the guards for the crucifixion.[7]

Pilate was not the first—or last—human to question the meaning, content, or value of truth. Throughout the ages, philosophers, theologians, judges, political leaders, and educators have wrestled with this subject. And it is a vexing question: What *is* truth? Thankfully, the Bible speaks abundantly on the topic. What does it have to say about the nature of moral truth?

God Is Truth

The most important and fundamental principle conveyed is that God is the essence of truth.[8] Everything that emanates from Him—words, plans, laws, judgment, blessings—is a manifestation of moral truth. Given His nature, truth is an aspect of perfection and holiness. He is the source of truth, the definition of truth, and the gauge of truth.[9] The laws, rules, and commands listed in the Bible give us the guidelines we need to comprehend and carry out moral truth.

The Nature of Truth

God knows that His truth is the only truth. Its uniqueness is shown by its having stood the test of time—mocked, criticized, misunderstood, and abandoned by some, but still accessible and irrefutable.[10] Those who resist acknowledging that all truth is God's truth must respond to some impossible questions: What truth claim in the Scriptures has ever been proven false?[11] What truth is not God's truth? What significant moral principle is not found in the Bible?

God's truth does not change; it is what it is, and it will always be the same.[12] That unchanging character is one of the attributes that makes His truth so reliable and comforting for us. It is not dependent upon or affected by circumstances, feelings, experiences, or personal preference; it is knowable, accurate, and consistent from age to age, from context to context. His truth is genuinely transcultural and eternal. It is consistent with itself, no matter what the situation.[13]

Benefits and Impact

Truth does not exist in a vacuum; it influences our reality. Scripture points out that truth has various influences on our lives, most of which are beneficial.

Most importantly, God's truth sets us free.[14] Free from what? Free from the grip of sin and its debilitating effects such as death and separation from God; free from confusion and anxiety; and free from the grip of the world's standards and expectations. Many people miss this point entirely, viewing moral truth as a set of restrictions that hinder their behavioral freedom. Nothing could be more inaccurate. God's truth, designed to enable us to enjoy the benefits of godliness, removes the bonds of human disability and dysfunctionality from our lives. Moral law does not limit us; it allows us the freedom to achieve the full potential that God placed within us.

His truth enables us to experience a pureness of heart that is otherwise unattainable.[15] Crippled by the debilitating effects of sin, God's truth points us in the right direction, allowing us to imitate His own heart more closely and consistently.[16]

ATTAINING TRUTH

No matter how wonderful God's truths may be, unless we understand and apply them, they do us no good. Therefore God has made His truth not only helpful but abundantly accessible. First, He sent Jesus to teach and emphasize what matters to God.[17] Second, He protected the information and sealed the information through the work of His Holy Spirit.[18] Third, He has called millions of talented and supernaturally gifted individuals to teach those truths to many millions of other people so that the wisdom of God and parameters He set forth would be known and adhered to.[19] Whether that teaching comes in the form of sermons in a worship service, books, magazine articles, presentations on television or radio, Sunday school or cell-group lessons, or other forms of instruction, God has facilitated billions of hours of Bible teaching absorbed every year by people in this country alone.

Significantly, the Bible reminds us that the truth is available to those who honestly seek it. Those who approach the truth bent on rejecting it may fulfill their desires, but they will never fulfill their God-given potential. God informs us that those who are humble enough to hear and accept His truth will find it available and life-changing; those who resist it will be sheltered from it.[20]

Opposition to Truth

Naturally, Satan is committed to blocking or distorting God's truth. He hates God's truth and will use whatever means are available to undermine it from invading a person's heart.[21]

Sadly, millions upon millions of people follow the devil's deception rather than God's truths. Won over by temptation and sin, we often accept pleasing lies rather than the harsh truth about ourselves and our world.[22] Still rebellious in nature, we ignore the Lord's good and helpful messages in favor of those that are ultimately hurtful to us.[23] To make matters worse, God has no choice but to punish us for our rebellion.[24] Thus, we experience a double whammy: We get hurt by following the lies of the deceiver then pay again for our disobedience when God exacts His justice.[25]

Thomas Aquinas suggested that when people reject truth they do so for one of three reasons: It reveals personal flaws (in other words, sin), it is a barrier to achievement or acquisition, or it conflicts with what we wish was true.[26] The common reaction is to hate the truth, but as Aquinas noted, truth is always good in nature and we do not hate things that are good. The problem, then, is that we do not really know the truth. Jesus alluded to this when He taught His disciples that one great benefit of truth is that it sets people free—and it is difficult to conceive of anyone disdaining freedom.[27]

Challenges to Believers

God's truth comes complete with challenges to its adherents. For instance, believers are encouraged to love His truth, to obey it in all circumstances, and to promote it whenever possible.[28] Thus, we can see the importance of moral truth to God: It is meant to make us more like Him, but it is also a valuable resource that we are to defend whenever necessary and credit whenever reasonable.[29] It is not good enough for us to simply embrace the truth and follow it. We show how committed we are to God's ways when we have a single-mindedness about seeing God's truth made known in every place and time. It is not just the clergy and religious professionals who are called to champion His truth; that is a job assigned to all of God's people, including you and me.

WHERE DO WE GO FROM HERE?

Contrary to public opinion, moral truth is not a private matter to be decided by every individual according to each new set of circumstances. God's truth is absolute, authoritative, and accessible; if we live by it we will thrive, but in its absence we will suffer.[30] Our choices have consequences. The failure to recognize or acknowledge His truth does not change the fact that His truth exists, it is always right, and it cannot be altered or ignored without peril.

Let me suggest that we keep five simple insights in mind.

First, we must acknowledge that God has dictated absolute moral truth to us. It is clear, comprehensive, and universal. It is not open to editing or expansion.[31]

Second, every truth that we embrace must conform to clear biblical principles.[32] No authentic truth conflicts with the terms set forth in the Bible. Because all moral truth comes directly from the heart of God, God cannot contradict Himself. Any alleged truth claim that is understood within an equivalent context but is inconsistent with scriptural teaching is not moral truth. Like a horse that wears blinders to remain focused on the road it must walk, so should we remain fixated on the defined truths that God has made plain to us in the Bible. We may sometimes discover such a principle through personal experience, reason, or tradition, but it must nevertheless fit with biblical precedent.

Third, if we are to think like Jesus then we must love truth.[33] Grudgingly accepting truth is akin to rejecting it. Moral truth represents the very heart and nature of God, so to embrace it with anything less than enthusiastic appreciation and confidence would be to snub the Holy One who revealed the truth for our benefit. By owning and fully pursuing God's moral code we convincingly demonstrate that our relationship with God, through the saving grace of Jesus Christ and the internalized power and cleansing of the Holy Spirit, has matured us as lovers of the Creator who first loved us.

Fourth, every moral choice we make must therefore reflect God's moral truths. Every choice must show our determination to model His truth in every moral decision we make. There is no "plan B." Our sole desire is to do what brings honor, respect, pleasure, and glory to God. By living this way, we not only show the depth of our love for Him but also prove that our intimacy with Him and His ways has genuinely transformed us into Christlike beings.

Finally, we must go the "extra mile" in our zeal for God's truth by seeking and exploiting every possible opportunity to promote, defend, and teach those truths to others. Promoting God's truth demands that our attitude prove our earnest appreciation of the content of His truth and an unshakable conviction that anyone who joins us in embracing His moral code will experience a better life because of that choice. Defending His truth means we must be prepared to suffer the world's misunderstanding and abuse. Instructing others in the substance of His truth requires us to be so well versed in those moral principles and laws that we are always ready, willing, and able to instruct anyone who will listen to the contours and nuances of that moral code.

For us to follow the truth in all circumstances, though, we must know the Bible intimately.[34] Every moral issue and choice is addressed in the Bible and may therefore be acted upon with wisdom and purity—if we draw on the truth of Scripture. Because thinking like Jesus is not natural for us, it is crucial that we incorporate purposeful Bible study into our regular life regimen and unceasingly apply what we learn from that effort. Anything less reflects a halfhearted commitment to His truth— and a partial commitment to the ways of God's enemy. As politically incorrect as it sounds, moral truth is black and white: You're either with God or against Him on every moral issue of the day. Know the content of His words to us sufficiently to be capable of making the right choice every time.

Knowing His truth is imperative, but we must also muster the will to reject the seductive alternatives the world has to offer. This is warfare, and we can count on the enemy to imitate God's ways but twist them and to offer appealing but inappropriate options for consumption. Never accept a truth at face value; always filter it through the grid of Scripture, prayer, and counsel. Our enemy is clever and takes perverse pleasure at our falling for his lies.

Is God's moral truth an obsession to you? It ought to be for every follower of Christ. After all, our decisions are influenced by the accuracy of the perspectives we bring to every point of decision; we cannot make great choices if we are working with faulty information. And if our purpose is to love God, and we do so by honoring Him and respecting His laws and principles, then we must gracefully and gratefully bow to His revelation of truth in order to do what is right and appropriate in His eyes.

Part Three

PRACTICING A
BIBLICAL WORLDVIEW

Eleven

When the Rubber Meets the Road

H EY, PASS ME THE SALT, will ya?" Bill Westbrook asked as he dug into the sumptuous meal that lay on the table before him. He had arranged to "break bread" with his good friend, Ted Applebee, after church. The luxurious brunch buffet at a swanky hotel was an anomaly. Usually they'd each be home by now, making sandwiches and iced tea with their respective spouses, but a women's retreat had stolen their wives for the weekend, and the guys were more than willing to let the Marriott take care of them for a few hours.

Bill and Ted had been friends since they joined the same golf club a dozen years ago. The forty-something overachievers had much in common and had become very close.

"Sure, pick your poison, buddy. That stuff'll kill ya if you keep pouring it on the way you do," chided Ted. "Don't they teach you anything about health and body care at that church you go to?" The two were regular church attenders, but each was a leader in a different congregation.

"Sometimes I wonder about what they teach," was Bill's reply between heaping forkfuls of mashed potatoes and roasted chicken. "Today we got the annual dollar plea. It's the start of the church's fiscal year, so the pastor did his usual guilt trip on us about giving money— 'generously, cheerfully, sacrificially.' He's on this tithing kick, trying to get everyone to give ten percent of their income. Ten percent! What planet does this guy live on, anyway?"

Ted listened with a cheekful of roast beef and rice. Bill went on.

"With the cost of living these days, who but Bill Gates could afford to do that? Man, I've got a kid in college, a married daughter who still thinks I'm the Bank of Westbrook, and a wife who buys enough Mary Kay products to raise the GNP a full point. I'm already giving more than most of the people sitting there each Sunday, but the pastor still wants more, more, more."

Bill shook his head and plunged another loaded forkful into his waiting mouth. Ted swallowed slowly before grinning at his tablemate. "I tithe, you know," he said softly.

Bill's chewing slowed from ferocious to normal, and he eyed his friend with surprise.

"Yeah, I've been doing it for probably five or six years now," Ted continued evenly. "Frankly, I can't imagine not tithing."

Bill and Ted were a competitive duo. Their battles on the links, on the tennis court, and even in spirited one-on-one hoops had become legendary at their country club. So, not surprisingly, Bill took up the challenge.

"Okay, Mr. Preacher's Pet, how can you afford to tithe? You've got two kids in college, a house bigger than this hotel—and, I assume, a mortgage that corresponds—and a lifestyle that doesn't exactly bring Mother Teresa to mind. How can you sacrifice 10 percent of everything you make? You must be playing loose with the numbers."

Ted smiled and said it was a matter of fundamental beliefs.

"Since our church went on this worldview kick when the new pastor came on board, my thinking and choices have changed on a lot of key matters. Tithing is just one of them. But it stems from a basic biblical perspective of how life works and what God expects of me—and what I can do to please Him. Tithing is one consideration that I understand quite differently today than I used to, and consequently my choices in regard to money are different."

Bill, a highly regarded city attorney, was intrigued by the direction of the conversation. "But Ted, tithing isn't taught anywhere in the New Testament. It's an Old Testament concept, carried over from the period when people were strictly under the Law. Jesus freed us from that—and I know it's odd to hear an attorney say it's good to be liberated from the law. But in this case it makes all the difference. The New Testament challenges us to give as generously as we can, but it does not shackle us with a percentage."

Between bites Ted beamed at Bill. Either he suddenly realized he was out of his league arguing with a prosecutor or he had lured his longtime buddy into a trap. "Bill, it's not a matter of proof-texting, you know, picking out a verse here and there to support your desired outcome. This has to be understood in a much larger context—the context of a comprehensive understanding of scriptural principles."

Bill encouraged his partner to continue. "Okay, so what's the argument?"

Ted washed down his latest culinary casualty with a healthy swig of soda then continued. "Let's start at the beginning. We both agree that God exists and that He created everything in the universe, right?" Bill nodded as if to say, *Yeah, that's no big revelation.* "Yup, but why did He do that? Well, it seems He created the world for His enjoyment and that He created *us* in order to have a genuine, fulfilling relationship with us. He wants to be loved, but He can't be loved if He forces us to love Him, making us like robotic slaves. We have to freely choose to love Him and have to demonstrate that choice through our behavior. Consequently, real success or meaning in life comes from knowing, pleasing, and honoring Him. You with me so far?"

Bill continued to inhale the well-prepared meal that was rapidly vanishing from sight. He waved his fork in the air while chewing, like a conductor urging the string section to speed up the chorus.

"Well, then, what would it take to fulfill our role in this relationship, to really love Him? To answer that we have to explore what He is like since we're created in His image and supposed to imitate His holiness and His purposes. Describing His character is when we encounter all the big words—you know, omniscience, omnipotence, omnipresent, immutable, transcendent. Seminary talk."

The two shared a chuckle at the secret-speak that clergy sometimes lapse into. Understanding those characteristics helps people recognize what's expected of them, Ted continued.

"If we are supposed to imitate Him, then those characteristics are the key to being people who bring Him pleasure. But we also have to consider our life context. When God created the world, He did so with the expectation that we would manage His creation for Him, with His ends in mind. So we are to view things from His vantage point and carry out His expressed commands while also recognizing unspecified responsibilities we have as a result of imitating His nature, pursuing His desired results, and striving to do whatever it takes to love Him."

Ted said we can best understand how to do that because of the Bible. It's the source of truth—the only reliable standard of absolute moral and ethical truth. It gives ample direction regarding how to perceive and respond to the world, he said.

Bill's legal mind was in gear now, putting the pieces of Ted's brief in their logical place. So far, nothing Bill had heard raised any theological red flags in his mind; he'd heard it before, although not necessarily woven together in this fashion.

"So what about money?" Bill asked.

Ted continued, forgetting the food on his plate. "The idea behind tithing is not that I have to grudgingly give a set percentage of my income to the Church. More properly, I have to understand that the Church is God's means of connecting His people into a spiritual family. Just as I have a responsibility to Justine, Chelsea, and T.J.," he said, referring to his wife and children, "so do I have a responsibility to my spiritual family. And it's not really sacrificial giving because these resources are not mine anyway.

They're God's, and I'm just administering His estate in His physical absence. What kind of sacrifice is it for me to give away someone else's money? No, as a believer, I have been appointed as temporary guardian of His estate, but I will be held responsible for how I dole out His funds. He trusts me to do what's right in His stead, but that means I have to reflect His values, His characteristics, and His choices as best I can."

Bill had ceased eating at this point. He was leaning forward on his elbows, a glass of Coke in one hand and a linen napkin in the other, intensely looking into his friend's eyes as he spoke. Unconsciously, he was aware of the significance of what his trusted comrade was detailing.

Then Ted brought up the other player in the picture.

"At the same time I'm going through these mental gyrations of trying to figure out how God can be most satisfied with my choices of how to use His resources, Satan is tugging at my ear, trying to get me to waste those same resources so that God is disappointed and His purposes are thwarted."

Satan would like nothing more than for people to believe that the guidelines in the Old Testament are antiquated and meaningless today, Ted explained, because then they have greater latitude to abuse the freedoms won through Christ's death and resurrection. But just as the Ten Commandments are still relevant, although not eternally binding, they provide guidance and measures of holiness that can help us focus on how to become more Christlike.

"I agree with you, Bill; there's nothing in Scripture that mandates giving exactly 10 percent of your income for kingdom purposes. But my interpretation is that the Old Testament gives me a sense of what God is seeking, and the New Testament gives me the leeway and encouragement to *exceed* that standard because I am no longer under legalistic requirements. I give a tithe—and some years we wind up giving more—because I believe that's what God would want and it gives me pleasure to do simple things—like giving away what is His anyway—in the belief that He is honored by such behavior."

Unable to restrain himself any longer from launching the counter-attack, Bill began his cross-examination: "So you think you will be rewarded because you're being a more generous person than others?"

"No, Bill, you're missing the point," parried Ted while pausing to take a gulp of his drink. "This isn't about rewards. Eternal life in God's presence, because of Christ's death on my behalf, is the reward. Geez, how much more of a reward could I possibly want besides *that?*

"Nope, I tithe because I have been loved first by God, I have been created to love Him, He has placed me in a situation in which I have opportunities to prove my love by my actions, and I can't believe how easy it is to please Him in this regard. I don't deserve any of the things I have, even the money I like to think I work so hard to earn. We both know that other people work just as hard as we do but have nothing to show for it. The money I have is God's gift to me, given in love. In response, my gift to Him is to use it in ways that make Him happy and joyful, which is a sign of my love for Him."

Salvation is not dependent on tithing, Ted said. "But my spiritual transformation, which took a radical turn for the better once I embraced Jesus as my Savior and confessed my sinful nature, is demonstrated by the fact that I can now freely and without worry give up what the world says I ought to hold close. Tithing is not a big deal for me financially, but it's a big deal for me spiritually because it shows to whom I give allegiance, the depth of my commitment to God's ways, and the spiritual transformation that is allowing me to see and react to the world differently than would normally be the case."

Bill tried a different tack to explore the soundness of his friend's reasoning. "So what you're saying, then, is tithing is one of the tasks you have to perform to be a committed evangelical, someone who wants to follow the entire law and be a kind of super saint? Doesn't that seem a bit self-serving?"

"Man, I ought to get a consulting fee for taking you hardheaded lawyer types through basic logic," retorted Ted through a wide smile as his friend pretended to swat his head in anger. He reminded Bill that the principle had nothing to do with theological labels, with fulfilling the law, or with personal benefit.

"This is about love and obedience. That's why you and I walk the planet. We're given the chance to choose how to respond to the freedom, independence, and responsibility that God has entrusted to us. We can be legalistic and do what the Bible commands because we feel we have to or else face the wrath of a stern God. But that's not love in action; that's just fear. When you're driven solely by fear, you're responding to a dominating tyrant, not a loving, caring partner. Are we told to fear God? Yes, but not apart from an understanding of His extreme and enduring love for us.

"I could do whatever I feel like doing and claim that God will understand because I'm forgiven. But again, that reflects a heart that has not been changed by that forgiveness; it reflects a heart that simply wants to exploit that grace for selfish purposes. If I refuse to tithe, do I jeopardize my eternal security? No, but it also shows that I have not yet been radically transformed by a complete understanding and acceptance and imitation of His love. I think it indicates that I have not truly surrendered my heart to God in love; I've only surrendered as much as I feel I need to give up in order to receive what I want, whether that is salvation, reputation, or membership."

In the end, Ted said, he tithes because he believes it brings God joy. He believes it shows that he is not captive to the things of this world but wants to honor Him through every choice he makes. He tithes because he believes the resources God allows him to supervise for Him are supposed to be used to express His love to others. By donating money to the Church, or by supporting missions groups or evangelists, he is using His resources to advance His kingdom and serve His purposes.

"If my purpose for living is to love God with all my heart, strength, mind, and soul, and if I do that by knowing His principles and desires and by worshiping and serving Him every moment of every day, then I'm not driven by the preacher's guilt sermon or by the pressing budget of the church or by the need to keep up with the people sitting next to me in the pew. I do it out of love, respect, and obedience in the hope that this small act will be taken as a demonstration of love for the God whom I want to be like and whom I want to please."

Bill was still sitting intently across from Ted, his elbows on the table, the clenched Coke and napkin unmoving for quite some time. After a few more seconds of silence, during which the two men stared unflinchingly into each other's eyes, Bill finally broke his statue-like position by exhaling and slumping back into his heavily padded chair.

"Hmmm." Pause. "Wow." Bill nodded his head several times during another pause. "You got this from your church?" the attorney finally asked.

"Well, my church planted the idea of worldview development, motivated me and many others in the congregation to get busy on this matter, and provided some key resources. But even engaging in the developmental process doesn't mean it's a slam dunk. I've struggled to develop a worldview based on the Bible, and I'm still in process—always will be, really. But, yeah, I would not be where I am today in this journey if it had not been for my church guiding me into a deeper understanding of the significance of worldviews and how the principles it's been teaching me since kindergarten fit together into a comprehensive perspective on faith and lifestyle."

Bill raised his hand. "Well, you're an elder there, so you probably get a lot of spiritual coddling that the rest of the congregation never gets a whiff of. I assume there aren't too many in your church who think like you do."

Ted shook his head. "No, no, no. I'm pretty typical, really. What has made the difference is that a few years back the pastor decided that if we weren't teaching people to think like Jesus, then we were wasting people's time mimicking a bunch of hollow practices and mouthing a bunch of meaningless words, even if they were memorized from the Bible. That began a revolution within our congregation, with all of our programs changed and the expectations revised for every believer. As much as I sometimes like to think that I'm 'da man,' the truth is that I'm not the shining example to be placed on the pedestal for all to appreciate. We've got many people who are more skilled at this than I am and many others who are on the same journey."

Bill exhaled again and shook his head in a display of disbelief. "Okay, buddy, I guess that nails it. I've got to spend some time with you at your church, checking out how the process works and how to get people into such a process. I will confess that I am dog tired of having a congregation of people who know more Scripture than Moses did but fail to apply it. I think it's time we found out how we can get our church to help us embrace what you folks are doing to be able to think like Jesus."

"Sure!" Ted slapped Bill cheerfully on the shoulder—it's a guy thing—and gave him a toothy smile. He felt satisfied that he had scored some points with his intelligent and savvy counterpart. He felt good about motivating his friend to take worldview matters more seriously.

They returned to their plates, but not before Ted thought of one more thing to get across.

"You know, Bill, the beauty of thinking this way is that it applies to everything. We're just talking about tithing, but whether the issue is cloning, homosexuality, divorce, poverty, voting responsibility, media content—doesn't matter, pick any topic that requires you to make a moral, ethical or spiritual decision and it's all covered when you start thinking this way."

He said this new way of thinking changed the way he ran his business, related to his family, and even the car he bought last year. "Let me know when you want to visit the church, and I'll set up some experiences to get your feet wet in a hurry."

The money thing was still on Bill's mind.

"So you don't feel that giving up 10 percent of your income to ministries hinders you financially?" Bill asked as he finished his meal.

"Not at all. In fact, I have had fewer financial worries and pressures since I started tithing than I had when I just gave spare cash to the church."

"Great," beamed Bill. "Then I think it's only appropriate that you pick up today's tab."

Twelve

─────ତ୬─────

HOW YOUR CHURCH
CAN HELP YOU

As ted applebee, the businessman introduced in the previous chapter, discovered, a church can be a huge asset for someone who wishes to learn how to think like Jesus and to be supported in that effort. But as his friend Bill Westbrook was all too aware, many churches are not focused on helping people develop a full-orbed life lens that enables them to emulate the Lord.

Even though one of the primary functions of the Church is to equip people to be more like Jesus, and local churches should intentionally and strategically facilitate people's ability to think like Jesus, most of the nation's Christian churches are not on target in this regard.

My research and the related training seminars I do across the nation have shown me that most pastors believe they are doing a terrific job of helping their congregants develop a biblical worldview and feel that they have largely succeeded. Unfortunately, as demonstrated by the fact that only one out of every twenty adults who regularly attend a Protestant church possesses a biblical worldview, that confidence is misplaced. There is certainly a widespread effort to teach people biblical content and to encourage them to lead godly lives. But, as noted earlier, vital connections are not being made between the three keys to worldview living: knowledge, skills, and applications.

The good news is that our research reveals that few pastors question the importance of worldview training for Christians. The challenge is to help them recognize how far short of the mark we are and to get them to adopt different means of growing Christians who act like Jesus because they think like Jesus.

PRACTICES OF WORLDVIEW CHURCHES

I believe many of the insights gleaned through studies conducted by Barna Research among churches will be helpful in this transition. We were able to identify churches across the country already doing worldview development effectively. We found churches of all sizes, denominations, and locations that have proven to be successful at leading their people to deeper maturity through a process that results in transformed minds and hearts. Not all of them use the seven-question approach that I have advocated in this book (see chapter 3), but they all employ procedures that are similar and that produce the same types of outcomes.

By describing the common practices of these churches, we can start building a foundation for any church—including *your* church—to help Christians become increasingly capable of thinking like Jesus. The rest of this chapter will describe the characteristics those churches have in common—attributes that you may wish to promote in your church for the sake of facilitating the widespread adoption of a biblical worldview.

Intentionality

First, it is important to recognize that these congregations have come to grips with a truth that is often hard to embrace: Simply preaching good sermons does not result in people developing a biblical worldview.

The half-hour weekly lecture often contains the information that might be helpful in developing a biblical worldview, but simply being exposed to good teaching and preaching does not get us very far. If it did, America would be a transformed nation: We have tens of thousands of churches where good sermons are preached on a regular basis. Yet the evidence is overwhelming that preaching alone does not get the job done.

Churches that are effective in worldview development incorporate various elements into a complete plan of action that they relentlessly implement. Among the critical factors involved in their approach are the following.

From Big Picture to Details

These worldview churches all have a key strategy in place. They begin with a clear notion of the outcome they want to see achieved. Then they conceive of plans that move backward from the end point to the starting point, identifying the component pieces of the plan and relentlessly carrying it out.

Past experience has taught many of these churches a significant lesson: Always know what you are seeking to accomplish and then build a process around specific objectives rather than pursuing vague outcomes based upon agreement on generally acceptable practices and ideas. As in virtually every successful group endeavor in which some type of change is the goal, progress depends upon having a thorough and feasible plan based upon accurate information, insightful strategy, clear objectives, intelligent assignment of necessary tasks, and complete implementation.

These plans often include some of the following elements:

- The need to educate and motivate people regarding the meaning, absence, and importance of having a biblical worldview

- A process for mobilizing individuals into activities that consistently facilitate the development of a biblical outlook on life

- The provision of resources and learning opportunities

- The appointment of leaders whose primary passion and focus relate to worldview development

- The establishment of widespread ownership of the process among all leaders and across all departments and programs in the church, including the coordination of content

- Methods of accountability and reinforcement of people's engagement in the process.

Uncompromisingly Biblical

As the name implies, a biblical worldview emanates from one place: the Bible. The worldview-oriented churches we examined make sure that their people recognize that although other sources of information, experience, and reasoning may contribute to worldview comprehension and development, any perspective or application that does not conform to Scripture is deemed illegitimate and unusable. These churches make no apologies for the fact that their worldview process is Bible-based.

In my work I have observed that many Protestant churches seem to favor principles from the New Testament, abandoning the rest of God's Word because God gave it before the ministry of Jesus Christ. The churches that are most effective—and, I believe, defensible—in worldview development are those that see God's Word as a unified body of instruction, knowledge, and guidance, of equal value, authenticity, and utility. The old and new parts of the canon verify and clarify each other. They must be proclaimed in tandem, perhaps within a kind of holy tension, but also in a robust completeness of God's revelation.

Connected Foundations

Importantly, worldview-driven churches provide their people with Bible content that is always placed in a broad context. They do not teach lessons, preach sermons, or promote principles that are independent, stand-alone concepts: Every element of their worldview is painstakingly connected to every other element because the Bible teaches truth—and truth is a unified reality, not a series of disparate, disjointed ideas.

Pastors, teachers and all church leaders have the task of providing Christians with systematic teaching about biblical content. Every principle should be taught and applied in connection to every other principle, demonstrating the veracity of Scripture and its holistic nature. Just as pastors are often taught systematic theology in seminary, so should they provide systematic theological training for their congregants, translating the sophisticated truths and principles of the Bible into language and concepts that every believer can understand, accept, and personally implement.

A Consistent Framework

In this book I have recommended the seven-question strategy as a framework to help people organize biblical information for personal application. Many of the most effective worldview churches have developed alternative frameworks for their people. Some have hinged on Bible memory and application, a few have related to cultural analysis and response, and still others have been based upon a hybrid method of observation, dialogue, and experiential training.

I have concluded that the question-based method is probably the most effective because it forces people to think, to own the answers they come up with, and to translate the questions into personal applications. However, the more important matter is to adopt a framework that works—whatever the framework may be—and stick with it.

Because worldview development is a long-term, laborious project, a church must remain wedded to its process for the long haul if it hopes to see results. Changing the process every few years will simply derail the entire enterprise and possibly do more damage than good.

Full Integration

There is also another way in which these churches connect the pieces of a biblical worldview: through integration into every activity undertaken and sanctioned by the church.

Worldview thinking permeates meetings in which ministry decisions are made. Worldview considerations are uppermost in the development of lessons prepared and taught in various educational settings. Prayers reflect the comprehensive perspective of people who operate from a fully biblical worldview. Worship is more powerful because it is practiced in the fullness promoted by worldview thinking. Service efforts are more intense and passionate because the motivation is different once the activity is connected to a worldview. Even social gatherings among church people assume a different air because fellowship is no longer engaged in for the sake of fellowship but rather for a larger spiritual purpose.

Total Family Involvement

Here's an important insight drawn from the research: Churches that have substantial numbers of worldview Christians in their midst generally initiate the developmental process when children are four or five years old.

This makes sense. We know that the moral foundations of most Americans are generally in place by age nine. Waiting until the adolescent or teen years (or beyond) to inject proper worldview thinking is much harder than starting young since you then assume a two-fold task: *eliminating* the unbiblical, worldly thinking that has taken root in the absence of a biblical understanding of life and reality and then *filling* the void with Bible-based, Christlike thinking. These churches work hard to introduce age-appropriate lessons on worldview realities, taking into account language, skills, developmental theory, and other insights that enable them to craft a process that clicks with the emerging capabilities of each person.[1]

Further, such churches tend to enlist the aid of the entire family in the process. This is almost required if you hope to see progress; reliance upon the one to two hours per week the average family spends on a church campus—much of which has little to do with faith development—cannot be expected to compete with the fifty to sixty hours per week the average American spends engaged with the secular media as it communicates alternative worldviews.

To maximize this potential, many worldview churches provide age-appropriate lessons on the same topic during the entire week in each of the ministry venues provided by the church so that everyone in a family has a common theme on which to focus and parents have sufficient information provided to them to facilitate intrafamily engagement on the topic of the week. The continuity that results—both within the family and within the congregation—proves to be amazingly powerful as a developmental tool.

Addressing the Competition

Many churches believe it is important to protect their people from the teachings of competing worldviews. The most effective worldview churches, however, believe it is imperative that Christians be informed about what the competition is offering. "You can't identify and defeat an enemy that you don't know exists," was the response of one pastor at a strong worldview church. The objective is to sensitize believers to the viewpoints of other worldviews and to help them understand how those perspectives conflict with God's truths and principles. Instilling the ability to recognize alternative worldviews enhances an individual's ability to reject harmful claims and offers that come from those unbib-lical ways of thinking.

Some churches fear that exposure to competing worldviews will result in attrition as people find worldviews they prefer to that of biblical Christianity. Recognize that such a fear suggests a very limited trust in the power of God and His truth. Worldview churches look forward to displaying the arguments of competitive perspectives because they invari-ably find that when every alternative is given fair consideration, God's truth always emerges as the most reasonable and compelling option.

A Balanced Approach

Too many churches think that we will win the worldview battle by providing believers with all the knowledge they can handle. The most effective ministries have learned that genuine worldview development is like a three-legged stool: Remove any one of the legs and the stool cannot stand. What are those legs? *Information, skills,* and *application.*

You cannot have a viable worldview without comprehensive, consistent, and accurate *information.* To possess a biblical worldview, that information must come from or, at the very least, be completely consistent with, biblical teaching. That information is more than mere factual regurgitation: For the information to have power, it must be understood and embraced as personal truth.

People must be taught *skills* to develop, maintain, and utilize their worldview. Such skills include Bible study techniques, memorization, logic, and critical thinking. These abilities will be used in both "offensive" and "defensive" ways as they reflect on their worldview and the alternatives. If we do not give people these basic tools, they cannot make headway.

Without *application,* a worldview is simply the intellectualization of reality—a head game we play that has no bearing on who we are, what difference our life makes, or how we relate to God. In order for people to apply what they discover about what it means to think like Jesus, a church must motivate people to engage in the process; build up their courage and self-confidence to be Christlike in thought, word, and deed; and provide supervised opportunities to apply their thinking in real-world situations.

As an aside, it seems that churches typically create their own resources for helping their people to make progress in their worldview. There are an increasing number of worldview resources being developed for the Christian market, but to date few have the combination of accessibility, breadth, and depth that make them indispensable tools. The challenge, then, is for churches to create their own resources that are coordinated across age groups, programs, and ministry foci in order to help people get where they need to go.

Connecting with the Culture

Nobody develops his or her worldview within a social vacuum. It is always constructed within the context of culture—the information, practices, and conditions that provide meaning and identity to a group of people. A fundamental challenge to a Christian, however, is not simply to develop a worldview that is intellectually solid or one that is spiritually defensible but to arrive at a worldview that both engages and transcends the culture.

To engage the culture means that we develop our perspective within the confines of the world in which God has placed us. The world is our context for experiencing Him and for ministering to others. We cannot afford to abandon culture, no matter how decrepit it may be; we are, after all, supposed to be the light in the darkness. That light loses some of its effect if it only shines in the presence of other light; it has its greatest and most memorable influence when it illumines an otherwise dark environment. Our biblical distinctives, then, must not only shape our worldview but also influence the culture in which we possess that life lens. This requires us to think like Jesus, not only when we are in the safe surroundings of the church campus, but also when we are in the scary and threatening surroundings of the world at large.

To transcend the culture means that we must not simply strive to fit in with the existing social framework but must utilize our worldview as a mechanism that lifts us beyond the decadence and ordinariness of the world. Wherever Jesus went, things were never the same; when He left a place, a piece of Him stayed there because of His transforming presence. When we demonstrate a biblical worldview, a similar effect should be evident: People will never view reality—or *you*—the same. We do not want to innocuously blend in with the environment; our job is to forever infect that environment with a love and appreciation for the transcendent God who created that time and space and who reigns as its Master. As His servants, we hope to bring others along with us on the journey of transformation, elevating them and us above and beyond the mundane to a more exciting, compelling and holy place within reality.

Realize that if you simply engage the culture but do not transcend it, you have become just another option for its consideration, failing to give it good reason to take the Christian alternative seriously. If you transcend the culture without truly engaging it in the process, you become a self-absorbed, arrogant isolationist, abdicating key kingdom responsibilities and privileges in favor of personal enhancement.

To engage and transcend the culture, you must take risks, blaze new trails, and experience both success and failure. Your church can become not only a significant training grounds on how to do this and a place that opens up new doors and windows, but also a safe haven to retreat to during the ebb and flow of your efforts to impact the world as you think like Jesus and act accordingly.

Leadership Is Critical

For the process to work, it must be made the heartbeat of the church, not a supplemental program. To enable this, successful worldview churches have a high-profile, authoritative, credible individual who serves as the champion of the process. More often than not, that person is the senior pastor: a person who understands the significance of thinking like Jesus, who has the position and the passion to promote the process, and who can keep people focused on this outcome as a hallmark of the church's efficacy.

The *champion*, whomever it may be, must ensure that worldview development is viewed as an "official" stance and purpose of the church and that it has the unquestioned stamp of approval of the ministry. These champions are most effective when they go beyond lip service to modeling the practice. In other words, if you want people to accept the worldview process as the norm, the trusted leader(s) of the church must "get it," and then they must joyfully and intentionally give it to those who need it. Until the church's primary leaders are on board with this process and way of handling life, they are not likely to fervently promote it, nor are they likely to motivate others to take the process seriously.

Anticipating resistance: One of the primary challenges to leaders who want their church to get on the worldview bandwagon is for them to anticipate the usual points of resistance to such a demanding process. If you have made any efforts to move in this direction, you have undoubtedly encountered some of the typical forms of resistance: rejection of the Bible as completely true and reliable, intellectual laziness, personal busyness, disinterest in making the necessary commitment, absence of convictions about absolute moral truth, and so forth. Being prepared to address those challenges is an important part of effective strategy. The best worldview churches have thought through the objections in advance and have conceived effective ways of disarming such concerns and enlisting people's full-blown participation in thinking like Jesus.

Perseverance: One of the most important aspects of leadership related to worldview development is perseverance. This is a lifelong journey, not a one-year or even a five-year special program. This is the foundation of spiritual training and renewal; it is never complete, and it should not be seen as the latest and greatest program. The highly effective congregations have made allegiance to worldview process to be one of the necessary conditions to acceptance as a lay leader or staff member. Solidarity among leaders is critical for the process to remain active and transformational.

Evaluating Progress

The more your church enables you to have a sense of how well you're doing, the more capable you will be of advancing your development efficiently and effectively. The effective churches provide their people with multiple forms of feedback: input based on behavioral observation and evaluative conversations; encouragement to gain insight through interaction within small groups in which worldview accountability is an expressed purpose of the meetings and relationships; and the provision for or administration of standardized diagnostics.

Unspoken Lessons

Worldview churches will sometimes surprise you. For instance, one of the unexpected lessons revealed by my research is that your church need not make constant verbal references to its worldview development effort. Even though effective churches construct their entire discipleship and education process around worldview facilitation, they rarely use terms such as "biblical worldview" publicly and only infrequently draw people's attention to the process and the goal. In other words, your church can make this work without being overt about the process.

Similarly, churches that pursue worldview development must be ready to realize results in the long term. Many of the effective churches in this genre indicated that it took a good five years—and, in a few cases, several years longer—before they began to see any appreciable and growing degree of results. Because worldview development is about transformation and generally entails replacing entrenched, errant perspectives with somewhat elusive biblical views, this ministry thrust is rarely described as an overnight success. If your church is going to engage in this endeavor, be sure it is prepared for the long haul on returns.

YOUR ROLE IN THE PROCESS

You might wonder what your role, as just one person in a church, could be toward facilitating some of these outcomes. In all likelihood, you are part of a church where the pastor and staff believe that worldview development is already in place and doing well. Making the argument that things could be improved, much less in need of a radical overhaul, may not be accepted with warmth and grace.

Building a Coalition

My suggestion to you is that you approach this as a coalition builder. Begin by talking to other church members you know who might have an interest in going deeper in their faith and learning how to think like Jesus. Help them to see the difference between knowing about Christianity and being Christlike, and make the connection between the latter outcome and receiving training in worldview development. Describe the types of applications and implications of possessing a biblical worldview, and begin to build sincere interest in church-driven ministries that will upgrade your ability to get the training and support you need.

Once you have a respectable coalition of active laypersons who are willing to request the help of the church, request a private meeting with the pastor to outline your interests and any suggestions regarding how the church could bless its people through worldview training. Because church leaders usually are overcommitted already, and given their assumption that they have been doing a solid job of facilitating worldview development, the more specific your suggestions are and the more "turnkey" a process you can recommend, the more likely it is that your request will gain acceptance.

To offer a turnkey solution—that is, a ready-made approach that will fit the church's culture and will not require oodles of hours from the pastor to build a viable training program as well as a shifting of staff priorities to facilitate that process—consider using some of the resources and services identified in Appendix 1 of this book. Join with several qualified leaders within your congregation who are entrepreneurial and strategic to develop a well-conceived and viable plan for introducing and sustaining a worldview process within your church. Model the plan on the attributes of the churches that are already implementing this approach effectively. Why reinvent the process when other churches have figured it out and I've done much of your homework for you? Use your resources efficiently to get a valuable worldview training process operational quickly.

Keep in mind that it is not your church's job to force you to pursue a biblical worldview. It is the church's job to expose you to the contours of worldview thinking and options, to equip you to develop a biblical worldview, and to encourage you to aggressively examine and refine your worldview. How zealously you pursue this outcome is your responsibility.

BATTLE READY

Your ability to fight the good fight in the spiritual battle in which you are immersed is largely dependent upon the mind-set you bring to the battlefront. America's Christians are generally battle tested, but rarely are they truly battle ready. We need better training and ammunition to wage an effective battle. Allow your church to provide you with the support you need to fight the battle with wisdom and assurance.

Thirteen

Being Transformed

Every wednesday my two daughters attend an Awana program at a nearby church. They have met many nice children there, have learned many wonderful lessons and principles, and have been loved and nurtured by the teachers in the program. To the credit of the program, both girls look forward to the midweek meetings.

Unlike me, both of our girls have a terrific memory and can rattle off Bible verse after Bible verse. Recently, our oldest daughter won an award for being the most proficient student in her grade level at Bible memorization. They made the presentation of the award a special event, giving her a commemorative plaque and a few prizes in front of the entire complement of students and assorted parents. She basked in the moment of glory, smiling broadly as her peers cheered her accomplishment. She was duly proud of her hard work and the recognition it had brought her.

Yet, within an hour of returning home after the memorable evening, she was fighting over some insignificant matter with her younger sister. This struck me as incongruous with what had happened earlier in the evening and the impact that Scripture knowledge should have on her behavior. I sat down with our award-winner and asked her some questions.

"What was that verse you recited from Luke 10?"

Without hesitation, she reverted to mechanical mode. "Love the

Lord your God with all your heart, all your soul, all your strength, and all your mind. And love your neighbor as yourself."[1]

"Good. A few weeks ago you memorized Matthew 7:12," I reminded her. "What did that verse say?"

Like a bullet out of a rifle, she responded, "Do for others what you would like them to do for you."

"Good job, that's the verse. How about Matthew 5, verses 44 and 45? Tell me those."

She paused for a minute to flip through her mental file box of verses before grinning and reciting the words. "But I say, love your enemies! Pray for those who persecute you! In that way, you will be acting as true children of your Father in heaven."

I stared at her for a few seconds, waiting for the light bulb to go on. I made a face at her as if to say, *Well, what does that mean?*; but there were no signs of recognition. She just stared back at me, waiting for the next question to ace on this spur-of-the-moment verbal exam.

"Honey, you just proved to the world that you know a lot of what God taught us in the Bible. And we've been learning that the Bible isn't like any other book; it's God's lessons for us on how to live a life the right way, in a way that pleases Him and is best for you. The verses you memorize should affect what you do, right?" She nodded dutifully, waiting for the next verse to call out.

"So think about the three verses you just told me. What do they have to do with how you treat your sister? What's the connection between what God is teaching you in those verses and how you two get along?"

Her eyes narrowed a bit as she tried to determine if this was a trick question. After mumbling some nonsensical reply, she sat quietly awaiting the next quiz question. She was a champion at recalling passages of Scripture, but she had no clue how those verses related to her behavior.

GETTING TO "SO WHAT?"

I don't fault my daughter for knowing Bible verses but failing to understand and integrate them into her life. I had been derelict in my responsibility, as her spiritual overseer, to help her connect the dots. She had the raw material at her disposal but no blueprint or coaching that helped her know what to do with it. She could answer, *What does the Bible say?* but she was not able to answer, *So what?*

Most of the adults I meet at church have been attending for many years. They could probably answer the seven worldview questions adequately—but few of them have a biblical worldview. Although they are decades older and have had much more experience than my daughter, they are no more spiritually mature.

KNOWING WHAT TO LOOK FOR

Each of us needs to move beyond the mere recall of the right answers to the personal application of those answers in every situation we face, every hour of every day. How can you tell if you have a biblical worldview and are living a transformed life? Nobody can determine this more accurately than you can, but you have to know what to look for and have some standards by which you gauge your status. Here are a few factors you might examine.

Habits

Your life is a string of interrelated habits. The content of those routines is one of the best indicators of what you hold to be true and legitimate. In fact, if you want to understand how to think like Jesus, one good way of grasping that would be to assess how Jesus lived.

You will find that the first four books of the New Testament provide a useful summary of what He did from day to day. He lived a very predictable life because He operated on the basis of a worldview that identified His purposes, moral limitations, and imperatives.

Take some time to read through one or more of the four Gospel accounts—Matthew, Mark, Luke, or John—in its entirety, in one sitting. This won't take more than an hour or two—unless, like me, you get so fascinated by some of the things you're reading that you get sidetracked on your way from the first to the last chapter. Once you have read the entire book, write down the repetitive elements of Jesus' life. What did you find?

Now, do the same thing in relation to your life. Analyze your activity for each day of the past week. (If it's easier, you might do this over the course of the coming week. Undertake this type of personal debriefing at the end of each day, just before going to sleep, for each of the next seven days.) Include the kinds of conversations, the points of conflict, the commercial transactions you participated in, the daydreams you entertained, the media you engaged, the places you went, the people with whom you interacted—everything you can recall about those days. Then identify the behaviors that were repeated three or more times. Those are clearly part of your routine. Once you've finished that task, complete the exercise by comparing your habits to those of Jesus. What are the similarities? What are the differences? What do you learn about yourself—and your worldview—from that comparison?

Your behavior is a direct outgrowth of what you believe to be true and significant about reality. The behaviors you repeat are the core reflections of your worldview. How satisfied are you that your habits describe a person committed to completely loving and obeying God?

Time

Time is Americans' most precious resource; it is highly valued, nonrenewable, and extremely limited. How we use that resource tells us much about what we truly value in life. Jesus, for instance, valued time with God and time serving people. If you perform a time analysis for your life and choices, how well do your choices reflect a commitment to things that conform to a biblical worldview? What changes could be made to facilitate a lifestyle that coincides with the way Jesus might have behaved if He were in your shoes?

Character

The Bible discusses about four dozen different character qualities that are important to God. In studying those qualities, it seems that they can be categorized to fit within thirteen character clusters. Someone who is committed to thinking like Jesus will monitor and reform his or her character to become more closely aligned with the character qualities promoted in Scripture.

Specifically, those clusters relate to the following characteristics, with a brief explanation of a few critical dimensions of each cluster attribute.

1. *Faith maturity:* basing life decisions on faith-oriented convictions, striving to live as a true disciple of Jesus Christ, exploring the truth and basis of every aspect of your faith, and attempting to integrate your faith into every dimension of your life
2. *Trustworthiness:* possessing people's confidence that you will say and do what is right
3. *Promoting truth:* clearly communicating ideas, facts, and principles that are consistent with Scripture and help people to become more Christlike
4. *Wisdom:* possessing a healthy, deep-rooted, and growing relationship with and reliance upon God for guidance, maintaining a vibrant prayer life as well as a viable balance between the intelligence of the world and the ways of God
5. *Sensitive conscience:* sensitivity and responsiveness to the Holy Spirit, inner turmoil over sin, reliance upon the Bible for moral and spiritual guidance
6. *Virtuous morality:* scrupulously following the Bible's guidelines on sexual behavior, substance use, and integrity

7. *Godly demeanor:* interaction with people that is consistently sincere, kind, generous, forgiving, loving, respectful, and encouraging
8. *Controlled temper:* controlling your language and anger, demonstrating patience and reasonableness
9. *Appropriate speech:* saying things in love and avoiding words that provoke anger, mistrust, or negative perceptions of others, avoiding abuse of God's name
10. *Loving heart:* engagement in pleasing God first, commonly forgiving and serving people, enduring personal suffering or disadvantage in order to love what is right
11. *Proper values:* having primary goals that relate to loving God with all your heart, mind, strength, and soul, and living in ways that are consistent with scriptural admonitions and objectives
12. *Servanthood:* sacrificing for righteousness and the good of other people, taking responsibility for people in need, acting with fairness
13. *Humility:* having an accurate view of your standing, rejoicing in the success of others, refusing to manipulate imagery to gain advantage, acknowledging your limitations

Audit your character to discover how closely these attributes resemble who you have become. Jesus was capable of loving His enemies, serving His creation, and resisting temptations because of His inner strength and depth—in other words, His character. If you want to think like Jesus, then fortify your character according to the factors that God has identified for us in Scripture. The more your character reflects these elements, the more Christlike you become.

Fruit

The apostle Paul helped us to understand what the Christian life looks like by identifying the outcomes that spring forth from godly living. In his letter to the Galatians, Paul described what happens when we release the entirety of our life to the Holy Spirit and allow His power to transform us. The results—*love, joy, peace, patience, kindness, goodness, faithfulness, gentleness,* and *self-control*—define a true disciple. Paul reminded his readers that to achieve these qualities we must "follow the Holy Spirit's leading in every part of our lives."[2]

Assess yourself in relation to these qualities. None of us ever perfectly reflects them, but there should be ample evidence of movement from one end of the scale toward the outcomes listed by Paul. Holding fast to the truths inherent in a biblical worldview should nudge you ever closer to becoming a person known for such attributes.

DISTINCTIONS WITHIN THE BODY OF BELIEVERS

As I travel across the nation teaching in churches and seminaries, one of the frequent questions raised is, *Which* biblical worldview? At first, this inquiry caught me off guard: How could there be more than one biblical worldview if that perspective is fully based on God's words and principles communicated through the Bible?

After discussing this matter with various pastors and believers, I saw some disagreement among people who genuinely love the Lord and are seeking to live a life that is Bible-centered and fully obedient. People from various denominational backgrounds may read the same Bible passage and understand it differently because of their interpretive framework.

It seems that such distinctions can arise for several reasons: a different take on the meaning of the words; differences in understanding the context of the passage and its impact on the meaning; divergence in terms of the perceived relevance of some passages to modern life; and pure ignorance of various principles, perspectives, and applications of the text in question.

Some of these are of dramatic significance to how one views God's message and its intent for our lives. However, I remain convinced that no matter what angle you approach Scripture from, if your intention is to honestly understand and practice the truths and principles God has provided to His people so that we may lead holy and significant lives of love, obedience, and service, then the magnitude of the differences diminishes. The theological or doctrinal differences remain real, but their importance is minor in relation to the big picture God wants us to grasp and live within. I am convinced that what matters most to God is not your theological purity but your holiness: Did you make each choice with the genuine desire of pleasing God and doing His will?

Contrasting Interpretations

There are literally hundreds of examples of issues on which dedicated believers differ on the interpretation of biblical matters. For instance, think about all the divergent theories of what the end times will be like— each of those perspectives supported with a parcel of Scripture verses and contextual arguments. Only one of those perspectives is right. Does the truth about the end times matter? Yes, if for no other reason than the fact that God chose to include it in the Bible. However, whichever perspective you embrace will not have a huge effect on how you live each day if you have adequately answered the seven questions that enable you to think like Jesus. Your view of the end times will be icing on the cake, but the icing is worthless without the cake. Your understanding of God's view on the seven questions is, in this analogy, the cake.

Theories about the last days are just one example of where authentic believers differ. Views on the Christian's civic responsibility, the age of the earth, the existence of free will, the nature of Heaven and Hell, the viability of the death penalty, spanking as a method of child discipline— the list goes on and on. I believe God's challenge to you is to craft a worldview that is fully and reasonably defensible from the Bible. Don't stretch His truth to arrive at a position you desire; get to the place where His Word seeks to take you, and then accept it. Live consistently with that worldview.

When Christians Differ

But how should you respond to committed Christians who possess a worldview that differs from yours? Try these four steps as a response framework.

First, *acknowledge that each of us is limited* in our understanding and interpretation of Scripture, and thus none of us is likely to have everything completely right. The process of faith maturity indicates that you are constantly growing in your understanding. The day you think you know it all and have mastered the Bible and its integration into life is the day you have become fully deceived. A disciple of Jesus Christ is always a disciple, never the Master.

Second, *accept personal responsibility for the content and the application* of your life lens. God will judge you for what you did and why you did it; you are responsible for your choices. Others may influence you, but when you stand before God on Judgment Day, you will be assigned total responsibility for all of your ideas, conversation, and activities. Step up and embrace that responsibility; take your worldview seriously enough to proudly proclaim it to be yours as you seek to honor God in every aspect of your life.

Third, remember that we are *called by God to love others*—especially believers—no matter what they believe that is contradictory to our own interpretations. We are members of the same family of faith and, as such, must appreciate and support each other as best we can. Jesus loved you before you even acknowledged Him as Lord and Savior. His example allows us to transcend our limited human inclinations in favor of a more mature view.

Finally, *it is wise to interact with those who disagree with us* so that we can more fully understand their perspective and thereby examine our own views more intelligently. Our natural tendency, of course, is to avoid those who think differently. Charismatics avoid fundamentalists, mainliners avoid evangelicals, Wesleyans avoid Calvinists, Protestants avoid Catholics. What a tragedy!

The more you can see the Bible from the vantage point of other believers, the greater your ability to dig even deeper into your own worldview to evaluate its veracity. Those conversations ought not produce walls of defensiveness but paths of understanding that allow us to recognize the power and richness of God's words to humanity. Every time you gain exposure to differences in worldview, take it as a challenge to study the Bible more extensively, to pray more intensely, and to listen more carefully to the guidance of the Holy Spirit in your quest for God's truth.

THINK LIKE JESUS

To be a genuine Christian is more than simply believing in God or Jesus Christ; even the devil meets that criterion. Being a true Christian requires more than simply believing that the Bible is a reliable ancient document; many archaeologists and historians who are atheists believe that. To be an authentic Christian is to accept that God is the Creator of all things, the indisputable Ruler of the universe, and the One who gave us life and purpose—the purpose of loving and obeying Him, and of loving and serving other people, and of living in accordance to the guidelines He provided in the Bible and in concert with the power and guidance of the Holy Spirit that He instills within us once we surrender fully to Him. It is at that point that we see the world for what it is and invest our time and energy in trying to think like Jesus so we can behave like Jesus—all so that we might please and honor God.

If imitation is the sincerest form of flattery, what better way is there to express your reverence for God than to commit yourself to thinking like Jesus?

Appendix 1
———⟂———
Resources That
Will Help

During the course of my journey I have encountered a variety of resources and organizations that have proven to be helpful. You may wish to consider some of these as you hone your ability to think like Jesus.

ON WORLDVIEWS

Blamires, Harry. *The Christian Mind.* Ann Arbor, Mich.: Servant, 1963.

Burnett, David. *Clash of the Worlds.* London: Monarch, 1990.

Colson, Charles. *Against the Night.* Ann Arbor, Mich. Servant, 1989.

Colson, Charles, and Nancy Pearcey. *The Christian in Today's Culture.* Wheaton, Ill.: Tyndale, 1999.

———. *How Now Shall We Live?* Wheaton, Ill: Tyndale, 1999.

Holmes, Arthur. *All Truth Is God's Truth.* Grand Rapids, Mich.: Eerdmans, 1977.

———. *Contours of a Worldview.* Grand Rapids, Mich.: Eerdmans, 1983.

Huntington, Samuel. *The Clash of Civilizations and the Remaking of World Order.* New York: Simon & Schuster, 1996.

Johnson, Phillip. *Reason in the Balance.* Downers Grove, Ill.: InterVarsity, 1995.

McCallum, Dennis, ed. *The Death of Truth.* Minneapolis: Bethany House, 1996.

Naugle, David. *Worldview: The History of a Concept.* Grand Rapids, Mich.: Eerdmans, 2002.

Noebel, David. *The Battle for Truth.* Eugene, Ore.: Harvest House, 2001.

_____. *Understanding the Times.* Eugene, Ore: Harvest House, 1991.

Schaeffer, Francis. *A Christian Manifesto.* Wheaton, Ill.: Crossway, 1981.

_____. *The Complete Works of Francis A. Schaeffer.* Vols. 1–5. Wheaton, Ill.: Crossway, 1982.

Sire, James. *The Universe Next Door.* Downers Grove, Ill.: InterVarsity Press, 1997.

White, James Emery. *What Is Truth?* Nashville: Broadman & Holman Publishers, 1994.

ON THEOLOGY

Bilezekian, Gilbert. *Christianity 101.* Grand Rapids, Mich.: Zondervan, 1993.

Bloesch, Donald. *Essentials of Evangelical Theology.* Vols. 1–2. Peabody, Mass.: Prince Press, 1998.

Erickson, Millard. *Introducing Christian Doctrine.* Grand Rapids, Mich.: Baker , 2001.

Evans, William. *The Great Doctrines of the Bible.* Chicago: Moody, 1974.

Grider, J. Kenneth. *A Wesleyan-Holiness Theology.* Kansas City: Beacon Hill, 1994.

Oden, Thomas. *The Word of Life.* Peabody, Mass.: Prince Press, 1998.

ON APOLOGETICS

Geisler, Norman. *Christian Apologetics.* Grand Rapids, Mich.: Baker, 1976.

Grenz, Stanley. *What Christians Really Believe and Why.* Louisville, Ky.: Westminster John Knox, 1998.

Johnson, Alan, and Robert Webber. *What Christians Believe.* Grand Rapids, Mich.: Zondervan, 1993.

Kreeft, Peter, and Ronald Tacelli. *Handbook of Christian Apologetics.* Downers Grove, Ill.: InterVarsity, 1994.

McDowell, Josh. *The New Evidence That Demands a Verdict.* Nashville: Thomas Nelson, 1999.

Sproul, R.C. *Essential Truths of the Christian Faith.* Wheaton, Ill.: Tyndale , 1998.

OTHER PUBLISHED RESOURCES

Book of Catechisms, Ref. ed. Louisville, Ky.: Geneva, 2001.

Archer, Gleason. *Encyclopedia of Biblical Difficulties.* Grand Rapids, Mich.: Zondervan, 1982.

Comfort, Philip, ed. *The Origin of the Bible.* Wheaton, Ill.: Tyndale, 1992.

Howard Center for Christian Studies. *Kingdom Living.* Dallas: Park Cities Baptist Church, 2002.

Niebuhr, H. Richard. *Christ and Culture.* New York: Harper and Row, 1951.

The Noah Plan. San Francisco: Foundation for Christian Education, 1997.

Oden, Thomas. *John Wesley's Scriptural Christianity.* Grand Rapids, Mich.: Zondervan, 1994.

Outler, Albert (editor). *John Wesley.* New York: Oxford University Press, 1964.

Schanzenbach, Donald. *Advancing the Kingdom.* Minneapolis: River City, 2001.

Stott, John. *Understanding the Bible.* Grand Rapids, Mich.: Zondervan, 1976.

Thorsen, Donald. *The Wesleyan Quadrilateral.* Nappanee, Ind.: Francis Asbury, 1997.

TRAINING PROGRAMS AND EXPERIENCES

Nehemiah Institute, Chicago, Ill.; 800-948-3101.

Focus on the Family Institute, Colorado Springs, Colo.; 719-548-4560.

Summit Ministries, Manitou Springs, Colo.; 719-685-9103.

Worldview Academy, New Braunfels, Texas;. 830-620-5203.

Principle Approach International, Chesapeake, Va.; 757-686-0088.

Appendix 2

SURVEY QUESTIONS REGARDING
BIBLICAL WORLDVIEW

W HAT FOLLOWS are survey questions used by Barna Research to gather data regarding people's worldviews. The survey is divided into three different parts, each designed to determine the answer to a specific part of one's worldview.

QUESTIONS DESIGNED TO DETERMINE
WHETHER ONE IS A BORN-AGAIN CHRISTIAN

Have you ever made a personal commitment to Jesus Christ that is still important in your life today?

1. Yes.   GO TO NEXT QUESTION
2. No.   SKIP NEXT QUESTION
3. Don't know.   SKIP NEXT QUESTION

The following statements are about what will happen to you after you die. Please indicate which ONE of these statements best describes your own belief about what will happen to you after you die. Which comes closest to what you believe?

1. When I die I will go to Heaven because I have tried to obey the Ten Commandments.

2. When I die I will go to Heaven because I am basically a good person.

3. When I die I will go to Heaven because I have confessed my sins and

have accepted Jesus Christ as my Savior.

4. When I die I will go to Heaven because God loves all people and will not let them perish.

5. When I die I will not go to Heaven.

6. I do not know what will happen after I die.

7. Other (explain):

8 Don't know.

NOTE: A respondent is categorized as "born again" if they say "yes" to the first question and choose response option 3 above in response to the second question. All other response patterns classify the individual as a non–born-again Christian.

QUESTIONS DESIGNED TO DETERMINE

VIEWS ON ABSOLUTE MORAL TRUTH AND ITS IMPACT

ON PERSONAL DECISIONS

Changing topics for a moment, think about the choices you make every day. People make their decisions in different ways. When you are faced with a moral or ethical choice, which ONE of the following statements best describes how you decide what to do? In other words, which one statement best describes how you usually make your moral or ethical decisions?

1. I do whatever will make the most people happy or create the least conflict.

2. I do whatever I think my family or friends would expect me to do.

3. I follow a set of specific principles or standards I believe in that serve as guidelines for my behavior.

4. I do what I believe most other people would do in that situation.

5. I do whatever feels right or comfortable in that situation.

6. I do whatever will produce the most positive outcome for me personally.

7. Other (explain):
8. Don't know.

** IF THE ANSWER TO THE FIRST QUESTION ON PAGE 203 WAS "Don't Know," CONTINUE; OTHERWISE SKIP THE NEXT QUESTION. **

What is the basis or source of those principles and standards that you take into consideration? In other words, where do those standards and principles come from? What would you turn to in order to discover the appropriate principles? IF THEY SAY "God" ASK: Do you mean that you would expect God to speak directly to you or do you mean something else?
1. the law
2. the Bible
3. values taught by your parents
4. Golden Rule
5. God—speaking directly
6. God—other: _____
7. personal feelings
8. lessons learned from past experience
9. Other (explain):
10. Don't know

Some people believe there are moral truths that are absolute, meaning that those moral truths or principles do not change according to the circumstances. Other people believe that moral truth always depends upon the situation, meaning their moral and ethical decisions depend upon the circumstances. How about you? Do you believe there are moral absolutes that are unchanging, or do you believe moral truth is relative to the circumstances? Or is this something you have never really thought about? If so, is that because you have thought about this matter and have

not arrived at a conclusion, or because you have not really thought about this matter? Which statement below best describes your view?
1. Moral truth is absolute.
2. Moral truth is relative to circumstances.
3. Thought about it, have no conclusion.
4. Never thought about it.
5. Don't know.

QUESTIONS DESIGNED TO DETERMINE
ADOPTION OF FUNDAMENTAL BIBLICAL TRUTHS

These questions pertain to people's beliefs. There are no right or wrong answers, so please indicate if you, personally, agree or disagree strongly with each statement, agree or disagree somewhat with the statement, or you don't know

1. The Bible is totally accurate in all of its teachings.

Agree Strongly	Agree Somewhat	Disagree Strongly	Disagree Somewhat	Don't Know

2. I, personally, have a responsibility to tell other people my religious beliefs.

Agree Strongly	Agree Somewhat	Disagree Strongly	Disagree Somewhat	Don't Know

3. When He lived on earth, Jesus Christ committed sins, like other people.

Agree Strongly	Agree Somewhat	Disagree Strongly	Disagree Somewhat	Don't Know

4. The devil, or Satan, is not a living being but is a symbol of evil.

Agree Strongly	Agree Somewhat	Disagree Strongly	Disagree Somewhat	Don't Know

5. If people are generally good or do enough good things for others during their lives, they will earn a place in Heaven.

Agree	*Agree*	*Disagree*	*Disagree*	*Don't*
Strongly	*Somewhat*	*Strongly*	*Somewhat*	*Know*

NOTE: A person with a biblical worldview would be expected to strongly agree with items a and b; strongly disagree with items c, d, and e; and to choose response option 2 for the next question regarding the nature of God.

There are many different beliefs about God or a higher power. Please indicate which ONE of the following descriptions comes closest to what you, personally, believe about God.

1. Everyone is god.
2. God is the all-powerful, all-knowing, perfect Creator of the universe who rules the world today.
3. God refers to the total realization of personal, human potential.
4. There are many gods, each with different power and authority.
5. God represents a state of higher consciousness that a person may reach.
6. There is no such thing as God.
7. Don't know.

Endnotes

Chapter 1

1. Matthew 11:29.
2. See Matthew 4:–11.
3. See Matthew 9:13, 11:13, 12:40–42, 13:14–15, 19:17–19, 21:13, 22:37–40, 22:43–44.
4. See Matthew 12:3–5, 15:3–9, 19:4–9, 21:16, 21:42, 22:29–32.
5. John 6:38.
6. See Matthew 14:13.
7. See Matthew 4:2.
8. See Matthew 16:13–20, 16:23–28; Luke 2:49; John 4:34, 7:18.
9. See Matthew 26:36–42; Luke 18:1, 22:41–44; John 17.
10. See Matthew 5:21–44.
11. See Matthew 21:23–27, Luke 11:17–22.
12. See Matthew 10:5–39, Luke 4:24–27, John 2:24–25.
13. See Matthew 16:21, 20:18, 21:12–16.
14. See John 14:9–31, 15:1–16.
15. The scriptural support for these benefits promised by God can be found in Proverbs 1 through 8, Matthew 5, 12, and 18.
16. See James 1:25, Jude 1:21.
17. Some of the Bible passages you might consider are Matthew 7:13–14; Mark 3:11; Luke 13:24–25, 24:47; John 3, 17:3; Acts 21:23–24; Romans 3, 5:8, 6:23, 10:8–12; Galatians 2:17–19; 1 Corinthians 1:28–31.
18. Among the books that might be most helpful in this regard are Billy Graham, *How to Be Born Again* (Dallas: Word, 1989), and Charles Stanley, *Eternal Security* (Nashville: Thomas Nelson, 1990).

Chapter 2

1. In my research, being categorized as a "born-again Christian" is *not* based on claiming to be born again, and it is *not* related to religious activity (such as church attendance) or denominational affiliation. It is based on answering two survey questions about religious beliefs. First, born-again Christians are those who say they have made a personal commitment to Jesus Christ that is still important in their life today. In addition, when asked what they think will happen to them after they die, they say they believe they will go to Heaven because they have confessed their sins and accepted Jesus Christ as their Savior. About four out of ten adults and one out of three teenagers fit this definition of born-again Christian.

2. Baby Boomers are people born during the years 1946 through 1964. Baby Busters followed them, born 1965 through 1983. The Mosaics comprise the generation born from 1984 through 2002. The figures for Mosaics reflect only those individuals in their teenage years.

3. For more information regarding the relationship of different faith variables and lifestyle choices, see George Barna, *The State of the Church* (Ventura, Calif.: Issachar Resources, 2002), available at www.barna.org.

4. This exploration of alternative worldviews is based on the work of several authors who understand world philosophies. The works that have shaped this section of my argument include James Sire, *The Universe Next Door,* 3d. ed. (Downers Grove, Ill.: InterVarsity, 1997); David Naugle, *Worldview,* (Grand Rapids, Mich: Eerdmans, 2002); Samuel Stumpf, *Socrates to Sartre,* (Boston: McGraw-Hill, 1999); Gene Edward Veith, *Postmodern Times* (Wheaton, Ill.: Crossway, 1994); and Fritz Ridenour, *So What's the Difference?* (Ventura, Calif.: Regal, 2001).

Chapter 3

1. Romans 8:28.

2. My thinking on the questions has been significantly shaped by several key texts. Thoughtful, extensive responses to these questions can be found in these volumes: Gilbert Bilezikian *Christianity 101* (Grand Rapids, Mich.: Zondervan, 1993); Donald Bloesch, *Essentials of Evangelical Theology, vols. 1 and 2* (Peabody, Mass.: Prince Press, 1978); Charles Colson and Nancy Pearcey, *How Now Shall We Live?* (Wheaton, Ill.: Tyndale, 1999); Millard Erickson, *Introducing Christian Doctrine* (Grand Rapids, Mich.: Baker, 2001); William Evans, *The Great Doctrines of the Bible* (Chicago: Moody, 1949); Norman Geisler, *Christian Apologetics* (Grand Rapids, Mich.: Baker, 1976); Stanley Grenz, *What Christians Really Believe and Why* (Louisville, Ky.: Westminster John Knox, 1998); J. Kenneth Grider, *A Wesleyan-Holiness Theology* (Kansas City, Mo.: Beacon Hill, 1994); Thomas Oden, *The Living God* (Peabody, Mass.: Prince Press, 1987); Thomas Oden, *The Word of Life* (Peabody, Mass.: Prince Press, 1987); Francis Schaeffer, *The Complete Works of Francis Schaeffer, vols. 1–5* (Wheaton, Ill.: Crossway, 1982); James Sire, *The Universe Next Door* (Downers Grove, Ill.: InterVarsity, 1988); R. C. Sproul, *Essential Truths of the Christian Faith* (Wheaton, Ill.: Tyndale, 1992); and Donald Thorsen, *The Wesleyan Quadrilateral* (Nappanee, Ind.: Francis Asbury, 1990).

Chapter 4

1. This information is derived from a national telephone survey among a random, representative sample of 1,010 adults conducted in January 2003. The results are consistent with those that we derive in our quarterly national surveys that track the elements of the faith of American adults.

2. See Hebrews 11:6.
3. See Exodus 9–12, 14; Luke 1:26–38, 2:4–20; John 19–21.
4. In fact, during my ride in the ambulance to the hospital and during the time when I waited for the doctors to work me over, God did speak to me in a very audible way about some things going on in my life. He had my full attention!
5. See 1 Kings 19:12 KJV.
6. See Genesis 3:13, 6:13, 9:12, 9:17, 17:9–19, 35:1; Exodus 3:14–15; 1 Chronicles 14:14; Jonah 4:9; Hosea 12:4.
7. See Genesis 15:1, 46:2; 1 Kings 3:5–12; Isaiah 21:2; Ezekiel 11:24; Daniel 2:19; Acts 9:10, 16:9.
8. See Matthew 8:5–13, 27:54.
9. See Matthew 4:23–24; 8:3, 13, 16; 9:22; 12:22.
10. See Exodus 20:5, 32:34; Deuteronomy 7:9–11; Isaiah 13:11, 26:21; Jeremiah 9:25, 14:10; Romans 2:2, 12.

Chapter 5
1. See Genesis 1:26–27, 9:6; 1 Corinthians 11:7.
2. See John 4:24.
3. See Exodus 3:14.
4. See Deuteronomy 31:21; Proverbs 15:3; Isaiah 40:28, 46:9–10, 48:5; Psalm 147:4–5; Matthew 10:29–30; Acts 15:18; Romans 11:33; Hebrews 4:13; 1 John 3:20.
5. See Job 28:20–28; Proverbs 3:18–19; Jeremiah 10:12, 23:5, 51:15; Daniel 2:20.
6. See 1 Kings 3:10–11; Ezra 7:25; Exodus 31:3, 35:31.
7. See Genesis 1, Isaiah 50:2, Jeremiah 32:17, Daniel 4, Matthew 19:26, Mark 14:36, Luke 1:37, Acts 9.
8. See Psalms 90:1–2, 139:7–12; Isaiah 44:6; Jeremiah 23:23–24; Ephesians 3:21; Jude 25; Revelation 1:8, 21:6, and 22:13.
9. See Isaiah 63:10–11; John 16:13–14, 17:3; Romans 8:9, 1 Corinthians 8:6; Ephesians 4:6, 30; 1 John 5:7.
10. See Exodus 3:14. Also see Genesis 17:1, 35:11, and 46:3.
11. See Genesis 6:6, Deuteronomy 6:5, 1 Kings 11:9, Proverbs 6:16, Romans 3:19.
12. See Leviticus 11:44–45 and 19:2; Exodus 15:11; Isaiah 6:1–4.
13. See Matthew 4:1–11.
14. Leviticus 11:44.
15. 1 John 4:8, 16.
16. See John 15:13.
17. Psalm 8:4. See also Psalm 144:3.
18. See Exodus 9:27, Psalm 7:9, Ezra 9:15, Nehemiah 9:8.

19. Psalm 145:17.

20. See Numbers 23:19, Psalm 102:26–27, Malachi 3:6, James 1:17, 1 John 1:9.

21. Hebrews 13:8.

Chapter 6

1. Note that the only exception to this rule is God: He is not a created entity, so He had no beginning. In fact, He is the only element in history that has not had a beginning, and He is also the only element in history that is not created.

2. See Genesis 1 and 2.

3. In each new episode of creation, the account follows the same pattern: *God said* followed by *and so it was*. See Genesis 1:6–7, 9, 11, 14–15, 24, 26–30.

4. See Psalm 8:3–4, Psalm 104, Acts 4:24, Romans 4:17, Colossians 1:17, Hebrews 11:3.

5. For a more thorough discussion of the intelligent design argument, see William Dembski, *Signs of Intelligence* (Grand Rapids, Mich: Brazos, 2001); William Dembski, *Intelligent Design* (Downers Grove, Ill.: InterVarsity, 2002); Phillip Johnson, *Darwin on Trial* (Downers Grove, Ill.: InterVarsity, 1993); Phillip Johnson, *Reason in the Balance* (Downers Grove, Ill.: InterVarsity, 1998); Phillip Johnson, *Defeating Darwinism by Opening Minds* (Downers Grove, Ill.: InterVarsity, 1997); and William Dembski and Michael Behe, *The Bridge between Science and Theology* (Downers Grove, Ill.: InterVarsity, 1999).

6. Hugh Ross, *The Creator and the Cosmos* (Colorado Springs, Colo.: NavPress, 2001).

7. See Psalm 19:1, 104:2–29.

8. See Isaiah 43:7.

9. See Matthew 5–7.

10. John 1:1–3 informs us that Jesus does not simply know about creation; He was there and a full participant in the creation process.

Chapter 7

1. See 1 John 4:8, 16.

2. Luke 10:27.

3. 1 John 4:18.

4. Exodus 20:20.

5. See 1 Corinthians 10:13, Romans 8:28, James 1:2–4, 1 Peter 1:6–7, and John 14:16, 16:33.

6. We are expressly told to bless others in Genesis 12:1–3, and Jesus' public ministry was a testimony to what such a life looks like. Paul's letters to his followers opened and closed with affirmation and encouragement, even when the purpose of his letters was to scold them for inappropriate behavior. The

importance of meeting people's needs is woven throughout Scripture, ranging from James's exhortation to serve widows and orphans (see James 1:27) to Jesus' practice of asking what people needed and delivering it (see Luke 18:41–42; Matthew 20:32–33; John 1:38–39, 4:46–50). The necessity of being in a faith community is illustrated by the story of the early church, as exemplified in Acts 2:42–47, through which the believers won over the multitudes, and by the example of the apostles as they lived with Jesus.

7. Examples of such service can be seen through the healings in Matthew 8, the comfort He provided to Martha in Luke 10:38–42, and His providing for basic needs such as food (see Matthew 14:13–21). His death and resurrection are the purest model of spiritual service imaginable, although His efforts to share the gospel with individuals and with crowds, His frequent prayers for hurting people, and His teaching spiritual principles to the disciples and crowds were further examples.

8. See Colossians 3:12–13.

9. See Galatians 5:13; Ephesians 4:32, 5:21; Hebrews 10:24; and Philippians 2:2.

10. Ephesians 4:29 exhorts us to use words that are good, helpful, and encouraging. James 3:2–12 warns that we must work hard to control the tongue, for it is a source of great harm as well as potential blessing.

11. See Ecclesiastes 8:15.

12. Food is seen as an element of pleasure in 2 Samuel 19:35; 1 Kings 18:41; Ecclesiastes 2:24, 3:13, 5:18. Music is promoted as fulfilling in 2 Samuel 19:35 as well as through the Psalms and other writings related to David's life.

13. Marriage is esteemed in the Song of Songs and in passages such as Proverbs 5:18, 12:4, 18:22, 31:10; Ecclesiastes 9:9; and Ephesians 5:28,33. The joy of children is noted in verses such as Psalm 128:3.

14. See Romans 12:16, 1 Timothy 3:2, Titus 1:8, 2 Timothy 2:22.

15. Jeremiah 2:7 and Micah 7:14 are among the passages that address this.

16. Ezra 9:12; Psalm 128:2; Ecclesiastes 2:24, 3:13, 22; Galatians 6:4, and Proverbs 13:4 discuss the potential joys of work, while Job 20:17; Ecclesiastes 5:19, 7:14; Proverbs 11:25; and Isaiah 65:22 deal with prosperity and wealth.

17. See Ecclesiastes 5:19, Proverbs 3:24.

18. See Deuteronomy 6:2, 22:7; Exodus 20:12.

19. See Hebrews 13:5; Ecclesiastes 5:19, 6:9.

20. Exodus 20:5.

21. As examples of the worshipful lives of God's leaders, consider Abraham (Genesis 22), Jacob (Genesis 35), Joseph (Genesis 47), Moses (Exodus 3), Joshua (Joshua 22), David (the Psalms), Solomon (1 Kings 8), Josiah (2 Chronicles 34), Hezekiah (2 Chronicles 29), Isaiah (Isaiah 26), Nehemiah (Nehemiah 1), Daniel (Daniel 6), Peter (Acts 10), and Paul (Acts 24).

22. Jeremiah 32:39–40.
23. John 14:15.
24. 1 John 2:4–5.
25. See 1 John 3:24.
26. See Galatians 3:12, Philippians 3:9.
27. See Exodus 34:11, Ecclesiastes 12:13, Genesis 17:9.
28. See Joshua 1:8; 1 Kings 8:58, 1 Chronicles 29:18.
29. See Philippians 2:13.
30. See 2 Chronicles 27:6, Deuteronomy 4:1, Ezekiel 20:13, Leviticus 18:5.
31. See Exodus 20:6 and Deuteronomy 5:10; Exodus 23:22 and Leviticus 25:18; Matthew 7:21; Romans 6:16 and Numbers 15:39.
32. Romans 14:8.
33. Matthew 20:28.
34. Jeremiah 5:23.
35. See Jeremiah 17:9.
36. Psalm 78:8.
37. Jesus called the religious leaders hypocrites on a regular basis. For instance, see Matthew 15:1–7, 22:18, 23:13, 23, 25, 27, and 29. He criticized them for not knowing the Scriptures on many occasions. Examples include Matthew 12:3, 19:4, 21:16, 21:42, and 22:29. He labeled people fools, stubborn, and faithless in various settings, as in Matthew 17:17 and 23:17.
38. Galatians 5:22–23.
39. See Isaiah 55:8–9.
40. See Acts 2:41–47.
41. Ephesians 4:12–13.

Chapter 8
1. The Barna Research Group has been conducting surveys of this nature for two decades. While the statistics have varied little during that time, our national tracking measures in 2003 showed that 62 percent of all adults said they had not confessed their sins and accepted Jesus Christ as their Savior. Among those who describe themselves as Christian but have not embraced Christ as their Savior, only a handful believe that they will go to Hell when they die, and among those who are not self-professed Christians, very few believe they will go to Hell, primarily because they do not believe in the existence of Heaven and Hell.
2. See Deuteronomy 6:5, 13:3, 30:6, 30:10; Joshua 22:5; 2 Chronicles 15:12; Psalm 84:2; 3 John 1:2.
3. See Deuteronomy 4:29, 6:5.
4. See 1 Samuel 20:3, Matthew 16:26.
5. See Proverbs 6:32, 11:17, 22:25; Matthew 6:22.
6. See Psalm 19:7.

7. See Psalm 63:1; Proverbs 24:14; Matthew 26:38; John 12:27.

8. See Psalm 13:2, 31:7; Lamentations 1:20.

9. We are made by God to experience spiritual outcomes. Various Scripture passages explain the importance of the spiritual nature of people. We know, for instance, that we are made in God's image, and He is spiritual (see Genesis 1:27, John 4:24). God promises punishment for spiritual immaturity (see Jeremiah 9:25) and cautions us that we will experience death unless we undergo spiritual renewal (see Ezekiel 18:31). We are exhorted to pursue spiritual fitness above all else (see 1 Timothy 4:7) and are reminded that God has designed us to be a spiritual temple (see 1 Peter 2:5). The Bible has frequent statements regarding the necessity for spiritual renewal (see Ephesians 4:22–5:2) and to regularly seek spiritual wisdom and growth (see Colossians 1:9, 2:11). The apostle Paul exhibited his understanding of the supremacy of the spiritual nature by encouraging us to surrender everything for the spiritual benefit of others (see 2 Corinthians 12:15).

10. See Job 10:1, 27:2.

11. See Proverbs 24:12, Matthew 10:28, Isaiah 55:3.

12. See Romans 6:23.

13. See Isaiah 14:12–17, 2 Peter 2:4.

14. See 1 Peter 5:8–9, Matthew 4:1–11, Luke 22:31.

15. See James 1:13–14.

16. See Revelation 20:10, Matthew 13:39–43.

17. See Job 1:6–12, Matthew 13:18–22.

18. See 1 Corinthians 10:13.

19. See Romans 3:23.

20. See Matthew 4:6–7, Genesis 3:1–6, Exodus 7:12, 1 Timothy 4:1–5, 1 Chronicles 21:1, Mark 9:18.

21. See Isaiah 59:2.

22. See Genesis 39:9; Numbers 32:23; Deuteronomy 20:18; 1 Samuel 14:34; 1 Kings 14:22, 16:2.

23. See Leviticus 4:2, 5:17; Numbers 15:24–27.

24. See Numbers 14:18, Exodus 34:7.

25. See Isaiah 64:5–6.

26. See Leviticus 4:20–26, Numbers 6:11.

27. See Romans 10:9–10, Ephesians 2:8.

28. See Isaiah 53:4–12, Matthew 20:28, 2 Corinthians 5:21, 1 Peter 3:18.

29. See John 3:15–16; Romans 1:16, 6:23; Ephesians 1:7–9, 2:8–10; Romans 5:8; 1 John 4:10.

30. See John 14:6, Galatians 3:21–22.

31. See Luke 24:38–39, 24:44–53; John 20:15–18, 21:12–14; 1 Corinthians 15:5–8.

32. See Acts 2:38, John 14:17, Romans 8:23.
33. See Galatians 4:1–7, John 17:23, 1 Peter 1:3–5.
34. See John 10:36, 1 Corinthians 6:11, 1 Thessalonians 4:1, 9.
35. See Galatians 5:19–24.
36. See Matthew 4:1–12.
37. See 2 Thessalonians 1:7–9.
38. The Bible alludes to Hell in various ways. References include *Sheol* (a graveyard—see Job 24:19, Psalm 16:10, Isaiah 38:10); *Hades* (the realm of the dead—see Matthew 16:18; Revelation 1:18, 20:13–14); and *Gehenna* (a place of sacrifices to pagan gods, a place of eternal fire—see 2 Kings 23:10; 2 Chronicles 28:3; Matthew 5:22, 10:28; James 3:6; Revelation 19:20, 20:4). Descriptions of what Hell is like are contained in Job 31:12; Matthew 5:22, 10:28, 23:33, 25:46; and Revelation 20:14.
39. See Matthew 25:46, 2 Peter 2:4, Jude 1:7, Revelation 20:9–10.
40. See Matthew 5:29–30, 18:9.
41. God created Heaven according to passages such as Genesis 14:19, Acts 14:15, and Revelation 14:7. It is described as the home of God (see Exodus 20:22; Deuteronomy 26:15; 1 Kings 8:30; 2 Samuel 22:17; Matthew 5:34, 23:22), of Jesus Christ (see Luke 9:51, 24:51; John 3:13, Acts 1:2; and Philippians 3:20) and the Holy Spirit (see John 3:6), and God's angels (see Genesis 22:11, 15; Nehemiah 9:6; Daniel 4:35; Matthew 24:36; and Luke 2:15). That God rules in Heaven is verified in Genesis 24:3, 7; Deuteronomy 4:39; 1 Kings 22:19; Isaiah 66:1; Acts 17:24; and Philippians 2:10.
42. See Hebrews 3:1, 12:23.
43. See Jeremiah 25:30, Matthew 5:12.
44. See Colossians 1:5, 20.
45. See 1 Corinthians 15:46–58, 2 Corinthians 5:1–10, Philippians 3:21, Revelation 21:4.
46. See Philippians 1:27, 3:20; Revelation 3:12.
47. See Colossians 3:2.
48. See James 2:19.

Chapter 9
1. See Ephesians 6:10–18.
2. See Romans 7:8–25, 1 Peter 5:8.
3. See Revelation 17–22.
4. See James 4:4.
5. See 1 Timothy 1:18.
6. See 2 Corinthians 10:3, Ephesians 6:10–18.
7. See 1 John 4:4.
8. See 1 Corinthians 4:9.

9. See 2 Timothy 4:7, 1 John 2:13–14, 5:5.
10. See 1 Timothy 6:12.
11. See Luke 10:19.
12. See Matthew 28:19, John 14:26, 2 Corinthians 13:14.
13. See Psalm 51:11; Luke 1:15, 41, 67; John 14:17; Acts 2:4, 4:31, 7:55, 9:17; Romans 8:23; 1 Corinthians 6:19; 1 John 2:27, 3:24; 2 Corinthians 3:6; Galatians 5:18.
14. See Genesis 1:1–2, Psalm 139:7–8, 1 Corinthians 2:10–11.
15. See 1 Corinthians 6:19; John 14:17; Galatians 4:6; James 4:5; Acts 8:29, 11:12, 13:2; Romans 8:16.
16. See Acts 5:32.
17. See John 16:8–13.
18. See Acts 15:8; Romans 8:16; Ephesians 1:13; Acts 2:1–4, 38; Acts 10:45; 1 Corinthians 6:19; 2 Corinthians 5:5.
19. See Matthew 22:43; Mark 13:11; Acts 20:22; Luke 10:21; Acts 13:52; Romans 14:17; 1 Thessalonians 1:6; Luke 24:49; Acts 1:8; 2 Corinthians 6:6; John 3:6; Galatians 5:17, 22; Titus 3:5; Acts 9:31; Acts 16:6; 2 Timothy 1:14; Romans 8:5–6, 37; 1 Corinthians 12:1, 4, 11; Hebrews 2:4; John 14:17; 1 John 2:20, 27; Romans 5:5; 2 Peter 1:21.
20. See Luke 2:26, Acts 1:16, 10:19, 1 Thessalonians 4:1.
21. See Romans 8:26, Jude 1:20.
22. See Acts 7:51, 1 Thessalonians 5:19.
23. See Matthew 12:31–32, Hebrews 10:29.
24. See Psalm 148:2–5; Hebrews 1:5–14; Matthew 13:39, 25:31; Isaiah 6:1–8.
25. See Job 38:6–7.
26. See Matthew 13:39–41, 26:53; Hebrews 1:4–6; 1 Peter 3:22.
27. See Luke 2:13; 1 Samuel 29:9; Mark 8:38; 1 Timothy 5:21; 2 Samuel 22:11; 2 Thessalonians 1:7.
28. See Luke 15:10, Revelation 7:11–12.
29. See Genesis 16:7–11, 18:16–19, 22:11–18, 24:7; 1 Chronicles 21:18; Matthew 1:20–24, 2:13; Acts 10:1–7; Hebrews 1:14; Revelation 1:1.
30. See 1 Peter 1:12.
31. See Genesis 21:17, 24:40, 48:16; Exodus 23:20; Matthew 2:13; Luke 2:9–10, 4:10; Judges 2:1–4, 6:11–12, 13:3–13; Colossians 2:18; 1 Kings 19:7.
32. See Genesis 31:11–12, Zechariah 1:9–21, Luke 1:26–38.
33. See Zechariah 3:1–6, Luke 2:20.
34. See Matthew 4:11, 28:2; Acts 5:19, 12:7–10; Luke 22:43.
35. See Matthew 18:10.
36. See Genesis 19:21, Numbers 22:22–35, 2 Kings 19:35, 1 Chronicles 21:12, Isaiah 37:36, Acts 12:23.

37. See Revelation 9:13–15.
38. See Matthew 25:41, Romans 16:20, Revelation 19.
39. See Isaiah 14:12–17, Luke 10:18, 2 Peter 2:4, Revelation 12:7–9.
40. See Matthew 4:8, 2 Corinthians 4:4, Ephesians 2:2.
41. See Job 2:7, Ephesians 6:12, 1 Thessalonians 2:18, 1 Peter 5:8–9.
42. See Colossians 2:15, Hebrews 2:14–15.
43. See Job 1:6–12, 2:6; Zechariah 3:2; Matthew 4:10; Luke 22:31–32; 1 Timothy 1:19–20; 2 Timothy 2:23–26.
44. See 2 Corinthians 2:11; Job 1:7, 1:9–11, 2:1, 2:6.
45. See Genesis 3:1–6, Ephesians 6:11, Mark 4:15, Matthew 4:1, John 8:44, Acts 13:10, Revelation 12:9.
46. See 1 John 3:8, Luke 13:16, Revelation 2:10.
47. See Genesis 3:1–6; Job 1:9; Matthew 4:2–11; Exodus 7:12, 22:18; 1 Samuel 28:7–8; 1 Chronicles 21:1; John 8:43–45.
48. See Mark 9:18.
49. See Luke 22:3, John 13:27, Acts 5:3.
50. See 1 Chronicles 21:1, Ephesians 2:2, 1 Corinthians 7:5.
51. See 2 Corinthians 6:15, 1 Timothy 3:6, James 3:15.
52. See 2 Corinthians 11:14.
53. See Job 1:6; Mark 3:22; Ephesians 2:2; Matthew 6:13, 13:19; John 8:44.
54. See Matthew 8:16, 8:28, 9:32, 12:22, 15:22; Luke 4:35, 8:27, 9:42.
55. See 1 Timothy 4:1, Revelation 16:14.
56. See Matthew 25:41; Luke 8:31; Revelation 9:1, 20:1–3.
57. See Matthew 7:22, 10:8; Mark 9:38; Luke 10:17; Acts 16:18.
58. See Matthew 8:16, 8:28–32, 9:33, 17:18; Luke 4:35, 8:31, 10:17; James 2:19, 4:7.
59. See Acts 5:16, 8:7, 19:12–13.
60. See Romans 8:38.
61. Ephesians 6:13–18.
62. 1 Peter 5:8.

Chapter 10
1. See 2 Timothy 3:16.
2. See 2 Peter 1:20–21.
3. See 2 Samuel 7:28; Proverbs 30:5; John 7:28, 8:26; Ephesians 4:24; Hebrews 2:2; James 1:18; Revelation 3:7, 6:10.
4. See Romans 1:2, 9:33.
5. See Matthew 4:10, 11:10, 12:3, 19:4, 21:13, 21:16, 21:42, 22:29, 22:31, 26:31.
6. Many books have been written about the history, authority, and reliability

of the Bible. Among those that I have found to be readable and helpful are Josh McDowell, *The New Evidence That Demands a Verdict* (Nashville: Thomas Nelson, 1999); John Stott, *Understanding the Bible* (Grand Rapids, Mich: Zondervan, 1979), chapter 6; and Philip Comfort, ed., *The Origin of the Bible* (Wheaton, Ill.: Tyndale, 1992).

7. This exchange is recorded in John 18:37–38.

8. See Romans 3:4.

9. See Isaiah 65:16, John 14:6, Psalm 119:43.

10. See Proverbs 12:19.

11. An eye-opening and affirming resource concerning the reliability and accuracy of Scripture is Gleason Archer, *Encyclopedia of Bible Difficulties* (Grand Rapids, Mich.: Zondervan, 1982). Professor Archer devoted more than three decades of study to the alleged inconsistencies and inaccuracies of the Bible. After fair-minded and exhaustive study, he concluded that there are no moral, logical, or spiritual inconsistencies in Scripture.

12. See Jude 1:3.

13. See 1 John 1:6.

14. See John 8:32.

15. See Psalm 86:11, John 17:17.

16. See Psalm 25:5, 43:3.

17. See John 18:37.

18. See John 14:17, 15:26, 16:13; Acts 7:51; 1 John 2:27.

19. See Acts 17:2, Romans 15:4, 1 Timothy 4:13, Titus 1:1, Hebrews 5:12.

20. See Matthew 11:15, 25; 13:9.

21. See John 8:44.

22. See Isaiah 30:10, Amos 5:10, Romans 1:25, 1 John 1:8.

23. See Ezekiel 12:2, Jeremiah 38:15, John 8:45, Acts 7:51, Romans 1:18.

24. See Romans 2:8.

25. See Psalm 96:13; Isaiah 42:4; John 12:48; Romans 4:23.

26. Peter Kreeft, ed., *Summa of the Summa* (San Francisco: Ignatius, 1990), 447.

27. See John 8:32.

28. See Zechariah 8:19, Philippians 3:16.

29. See Jeremiah 9:3, 2 Corinthians 13:8, Philippians 1:7, Jude 1:3.

30. See John 10:35, 2 Timothy 3:16.

31. See Exodus 23:20–22; Matthew 5:17–19; John 8:14–18, 10:35, 12:48–50; 2 Peter 1:5.

32. See Acts 17:11.

33. See Zechariah 8:19.

34. See Deuteronomy 6:6–9.

Chapter 12
1. For more information on how churches can develop an effective world-view development process among young people, see a related book I wrote in conjunction with our worldview research, entitled *Transforming Children into Spiritual Champions* (Ventura, Calif.: Regal, 2003). In that study we learned that spiritual transformation is most readily evident when the church takes a long-term view of Christian education, seeks to achieve a biblical worldview as a key outcome, and integrates such an approach into a comprehensive approach to faith education.

Chapter 13
1. Luke 10:27.
2. See Galatians 5:22–25.